Praise for M.A.C. Farrant

"Farrant's ninety-three short stories, inspired by the 'puzzling,' are full of humour, irreverence and insights into the puzzle that is life." —*ABC Book World*

"I hadn't had the pleasure of being this entertained by a book in some while."
—Heidi Greco, *British Columbia Review*

"I'm devouring M.A.C. Farrant's brilliant new book, *Jigsaw*, which examines the puzzle of conscious existence with ninety-three pieces of inimitable perplexity – and cows."
—Pauline Holdstock, *New Quarterly*

Other Praise for M.A.C. Farrant

"Farrant is a trapeze artist of the imagination, swinging over the existential void." —*BC Bookworld*

"A master of the Zen-like art of delivering weight in a way that is featherlight." —Bill Richardson, author of *I Saw Three Ships* and winner of the Stephen Leacock Medal for Humour

"Delightful and disturbing in all the best ways."
—Diane Schoemperlen, *Globe and Mail*

"Quixotically brilliant." —*January Magazine*

"One of our most original and imaginative writers."
—Margaret Gunning, *Edmonton Journal*

"A writer at the height of her creative and intellectual powers."
— Christina Mansueti, *Malahat Review*

"M.A.C. Farrant is rapidly becoming a cult writer for her short fiction, written with perfect economy and with pungent and sometimes surreal irony laid on like thin coats of paint."
—George Fetherling, *New Brunswick Reader*

MY TURQUOISE YEARS

Also by M.A.C. FARRANT

Short Fiction

Altered Statements
*The Breakdown So Far**
*Darwin Alone in the Universe**
*The Days: Forecasts, Warnings, Advice**
*Down the Road to Eternity: New and Selected Fiction**
Girls around the House
*The Great Happiness: Stories and Comics**
Raw Material
Sick Pigeon
What's True, Darling
Word of Mouth
*The World Afloat: Miniatures**

Novel

*The Strange Truth about Us: A Novel of Absence**

Nonfiction

*Jigsaw: A Puzzle in Ninety-Three Pieces**
My Turquoise Years
*One Good Thing: A Living Memoir**
The Secret Lives of Litterbugs and Other True Stories

Plays

My Turquoise Years
Rob's Guns & Ammo

*Available from Talonbooks

MY TURQUOISE YEARS

A MEMOIR

Twentieth Anniversary Edition
with five encore companion stories

INTRODUCTION BY LYNNE VAN LUVEN

M.A.C. FARRANT

TALONBOOKS

Talonbooks
9259 Shaughnessy Street, Vancouver, British Columbia, Canada v6p 6r4
talonbooks.com

Talonbooks is located on xʷməθkʷəy̓əm, Sḵwx̱wú7mesh, and səlilwətaɬ Lands.

First printing: 2024

Typeset in EB Garamond
Printed and bound in Canada on 100% post-consumer recycled paper

Cover photographs courtesy M.A.C. Farrant

Talonbooks acknowledges the financial support of the Canada Council for the
Arts, the Government of Canada through the Canada Book Fund, and the Province
of British Columbia through the British Columbia Arts Council and the Book
Publishing Tax Credit.

Library and Archives Canada Cataloguing in Publication

Title: My turquoise years : a memoir / M.A.C. Farrant ;
introduction by Lynne Van Luven.
Names: Farrant, M. A. C. (Marion Alice Coburn), 1947- author
Description: Twentieth anniversary edition with five additional stories.
Identifiers: Canadiana 20240363531 | ISBN 9781772016369 (softcover)
Subjects: LCSH: Farrant, M. A. C. (Marion Alice Coburn), 1947-—Childhood
and youth. | CSH: Authors,
    Canadian (English)—20th century—Biography. | LCGFT: Autobiographies.
Classification: LCC PS8561.A76 Z46 2024 | DDC C813/.54—dc23

In memory of Nancy and Billy

For Elsie (1905–2003)

And for their grandchildren,
Anna and Bill

"It's simple," they say,

"and you too have come

into the world to do this, to go easy, to be filled

with light, and to shine."

—MARY OLIVER
"When I am Among the Trees"
Thirst (2007)

PREFACE

LUCK, GRATITUDE, AND ELSIE SEXTON

IT WAS 2002 AND I was having tea with Elsie in the co-op housing unit where she lived, having sold the Cordova Bay house to her daughter Shirley in the late 1980s. Elsie was the aunt who raised me, my father's sister, and she'd always had a razor-sharp skill in knocking me down to size – "so you don't get too uppity." On this particular morning the razor found its mark. There was a pause in our conversation and then she asked, almost as an aside, what I was "getting up to" these days with my writing. I said, "A memoir."

"Oh, whose?"

"Mine," I said.

She laughed outright, "Yours? What have you ever done to deserve a memoir? There's only one person who should have a memoir and that's Ida Clarkson."

The venerable Ida Clarkson. I should have known. Elsie admired her enormously. She was the star of *The Ida Clarkson Show*, which broadcast live every weekday noon on CHEK TV in Victoria from the 1960s to the 1980s. She interviewed women about all things domestic: home canning, sewing curtains, baby care, weeknight dinners, and the many things to be done with potatoes. She also showcased volunteering and "doing good" in the community by holding raffles and bake sales to raise funds for charity.

"You ought to be writing Ida Clarkson's memoir," Elsie said. "Now there's a woman who's done important things in her life. Had her own

TV show for thirty years, for Pete's sake! I think she even judged the Victoria Day parade every year, the bands and floats. Not to mention the beautiful clothes she had. Made them herself. She's retired now. I miss her show."

Never one to reach Elsie's blue-ribbon standard of domesticity – she was a master knitter and sewer and a wielder of lethal household chemicals – I said, "I will never be Ida Clarkson. Not in a million years."

"You got that right!"

"I am writing the Marion Gibson Show."

This incomprehensible fact kept her quiet for about thirty seconds. "Well," she said finally, "if I'm in it, make me beautiful like Ginger Rogers."

Ah Elsie, I now say, I have made you as splendid as I could, as beautiful as you were! Who else would take an abandoned, undisciplined five-year-old and raise her as her own? What incredibly good luck I had! Against all odds, she gave me the gift of a happy childhood.

My Turquoise Years was written in this spirit of gratitude – to Elsie, her husband Ernie, my boisterous extended family, friends from the time, and especially my father Billy, who oversaw my upbringing from Vancouver. Unwaveringly, he visited us every other weekend. We were a tight-knit family and though I was an anomaly for the times, a girl without a mother, I was never made to feel "different" at home.

As a writer of fiction, writing a memoir had never occurred to me. The book only came about because of my fortuitously bumping into poet and novelist Susan Musgrave one afternoon on the street in Sidney. She said she was editing a YA anthology about mothers and daughters and invited me to submit. I laughed then and I laughed in my note to her later. I did not have a mother-daughter relationship, I told her. In fact, I had a cruise ship–loving mother who was only interested in pursuing men and money, playing the piano in every ship's lounge, wearing dazzling clothes, and ignoring her daughter. Susan sent my note to the publisher, who in turn sent it to Rob Sanders of Greystone Books. He commissioned me to write *My Turquoise Years* for an adult market and I thank agent Carolyn Swayze for brokering the deal.

My Turquoise Years was published in 2004 and I am so pleased to be writing this preface to the twentieth anniversary edition. Again, gratitude comes into play. My long-time publisher Talonbooks and I have put together an expanded version. It includes five companion stories, some forty pages of additional material, that briefly saw the light of day in a book published by Key Porter Books in 2009. Four months after publication the press went bankrupt and all copies of the book were destroyed. I am happy the stories are joining the original book and now have a permanent home.

My Turquoise Years found a receptive audience. It was read by well-known West Coast actress Nicola Cavendish in a serialized version for CBC Radio. Nicola suggested I send the book to the Arts Club Theatre Company in Vancouver where she often performed. After reading the book dramaturge Rachel Ditor tasked me with writing the stage play, and after five years and a number of public readings, the play was produced by the Arts Club in 2013.

Elsie died shortly before *My Turquoise Years,* the book, appeared. She was ninety-eight years old, living independently, and still making her own meals (breaded veal cutlets on Mondays!) and dusting and vacuuming with the same furiousness she'd always practised. She remained to the end a commanding presence in the lives of her family members.

I hope she would have been appreciative and maybe even delighted with her portrayal in the book, the play, and now the additional stories. Besides my father, she was a profoundly important person in my life, a lovable, hectoring giant. Her voice is lodged permanently in my head and I can hear her saying of this anniversary edition, "Ha! Pretty good. But don't go around thinking you're better than the rest of us because of it!"

I wouldn't dare.

—M.A.C. FARRANT

INTRODUCTION

IT'S NOT OFTEN I happily reread a memoir published two decades ago. This is not because I dislike memoirs; quite the contrary: they are my favourite form of nonfiction. But I don't often revisit them because I am one of those readers always driven to seek the new, to read about some additional slice of life in order to better understand human nature and the challenges visited upon individuals. Memoirs offer readers an opportunity to better understand their own lives in comparison with someone else's – especially if that someone has chipped their own clear narrative out of the jumble of early experience. To my mind, the chance to vicariously live other lives – usually far more interesting than one's own – is one of the principal lures of the memoir, a subgenre of what we now call creative nonfiction.

All that said, the re-issue of M.A.C. Farrant's *My Turquoise Years* is a delightful development which will give a whole new generation of readers the chance to discover an irrepressible voice, a voice endlessly fresh and accessible.

My aunt hollered from the kitchen. "Marion!"

No answer.

"Marion!"

No answer.

I was a few feet away, lying sideways across my bed. When she flung open the bedroom door I said delightedly, "You sound like Aunt Polly."

"Who?"

What a brilliant memoir opening; in just thirty-nine words, Farrant distills the initial impetus for her narrative: the resistance precocious thirteen-year-old Marion deploys to be seen as herself, to be interesting and a distinct personality, and the way these tactics trigger her Aunt Elsie, her down-to-earth opponent, who is raising her. By dialogue alone, Farrant is able to capture the essence of her younger self: a willful bookworm in constant need of drama whose behaviour exasperates her pragmatic guardian aunt. The interaction between aunt and niece creates the ongoing struggle that shapes the memoir's entire narrative.

As in 2004, when I first read *My Turquoise Years*, in my rereading I saw again how Farrant's deft handling of voice – both Marion's and Elsie's – propels the memoir. And that skill remains untouched by the passage of time. When I complemented the author on that virtuosity, she recalled that each day as she sat down to write *My Turquoise Years*, she would reread her previous day's work, to ensure consistency within the memoir's chapters.

Farrant's subsequent work – the reissue of the memoir marks her nineteenth publication, not counting several chapbooks – has confirmed her to be a writer with a great eye for detail, an acute sense of humour, and an inherent love of language. All these traits are visible in the first chapter of *My Turquoise Years* when young Marion reports on her own character as seen through Aunt Elsie's eyes: "Earth, according to my aunt, was a place I was frequently trying to escape. She claimed I liked nothing better than to get on my high horse and stick my nose in the clouds."

Aunt Elsie, a doughty and efficient housewife in her fifties, is unimpressed with her niece's emerging character, calling her "overheated," "too smart for my own good," with "ants in my pants."

At thirteen, everyone said I was a smarty-pants, a smart aleck. A wiseacre. A pain in the ass.

I thought I was a barrel of laughs.

I suspect some of these descriptive phrases from the 1960s may still be heard today in households visited by intergenerational conflict.

Farrant says she did consider writing a sequel to *My Turquoise Years*, but felt that would be boxing herself in, "duplicating" herself. Instead, when the memoir's rights reverted to her, she approached Talonbooks about an anniversary issue – with five later companion stories added to the 2024 publication, "at the end, like an encore."

Looking back at herself in the 1960s, today's Farrant sees young Marion as "so dumb but so smart," and now realizes how fortunate she was that her peripatetic Australian mother Nancy left her sea-captain Canadian father Billy, enabling her stable, loving childhood with her Aunt Elsie, Uncle Ernie, and their extended family who "moved through life in a posse" and did everything together. Although she seldom saw her unreliable absent mother, her father Billy (Aunt Elsie's brother) visited her every other weekend from the time she was five until she was eighteen. He was a single father doing his best, with Aunt Elsie as his and Marion's anchor.

But a fine memoir cannot sustain itself on voice alone. Readers, once entranced, immediately want to know, where? Where is this intriguing life being lived? And when? *My Turquoise Years* is set on Vancouver Island in Cordova Bay, where Farrant grew up, in a bygone time (1960–1964) which may seem quaint to readers in 2024. Farrant describes it as a plastic-mad era when turquoise was the "it" colour and working wives were a faint shadow upon the horizon. At the time, semirural Cordova Bay was five miles outside of staid Victoria, which made it extra special to Marion, a safe landing after her turbulent early life. Farrant brilliantly evokes the freedom of a child poised on the brink of adolescence:

> On hot summer afternoons, agitated sand flies skimmed the sand's surface. I'd watch hundreds of them feeding on the rotting seaweed that was strewn, half-hidden, like beige rags in the sand; you could kick at patches of it and watch the flies swoop off together like a flock of startled birds. The sharp iodine smell of seaweed was a marvellous thing, pungent and rank; thick beds of seaweed floated near the shore at high tide, looking like the long green hair of mermaids ... Standing at the top of the bank behind our house, eager to be running free

with Rip on the sandbar below, I'd often feel exhilarated. By the light, and the brightness, and by the sense of endless space.

As all memoirists know, they are writing about a wedge of life, a heightened segment of their history which shaped their whole selves. Farrant wisely distills her memoir into four years, her life from thirteen to seventeen, using key anecdotes to show Marion's growth from angular tomboy, romping on the beach with her dog Rip and her best friend Doris, to a backcombed blond in a pink-satin gown and gardenia wrist corsage, dressed for a high-school prom. Despite her vigorous protestations, Marion has grown up, has developed "boobs," is interested in boys, and has become a strong young woman who can handle the disappointment of her self-centred errant mother's long-delayed visit.

My Turquoise Years ends, as all satisfying memoirs do, with its protagonist having endured life's buffeting and upheaval to come to a place of wisdom. Marion sees that she has "done the right thing to keep [Nancy] at arm's length, pushed away" all these years because Elsie has been the better mother, despite their spats, yelling matches, and conflicts.

—LYNNE VAN LUVEN

1960

ONE

Marion and Rip

My Aunt hollered from the kitchen. "Marion!"

No answer.

"Marion!"

No answer.

I was a few feet away, lying sideways across my bed. When she flung open the bedroom door I said delightedly, "You sound like Aunt Polly."

"Who?"

"Tom Sawyer's aunt. In my book ..."

"A book," Elsie said crossly. "I might have known. When there are supper dishes waiting. You've been in here for over an hour."

"It's a good book," I said. "You're just like Aunt Polly. And I'm like ..."

"Never mind that," Elsie said. "It's time to do your chores. Time you came down to earth."

Thud. She swept from my room.

Earth, according to my aunt, was a place I was frequently trying to escape. She claimed I liked nothing better than to get on my high horse and stick my nose in the clouds. My high horse. A lovely image, I thought, picturing myself astride a magnificent white mare galloping serenely towards the heavens.

AT THIRTEEN EVERYONE SAID I was an overheated child. That I made mountains out of molehills. That I was too smart for my own good. That I was a Miss Know-It-All. That I did too much thinking. That I was too easily influenced. That I had ants in my pants. That I always had to have my own way. That I had eyes in the back of my head. That I was a little pitcher with big ears. That I read the dictionary just so I could use big words that no one else would understand. That I was always doing harebrained things like putting on plays for the neighbourhood or building tree forts for wild rabbits.

And these, I liked to insist, were some of my good qualities.

The list of my bad qualities – alleged, of course – was just as long.

That I was spoiled and willful. That I believed the sun rose and set on my head. That I was high-strung. That I was secretive and sneaky. That I lied. That I wasn't as smart as I thought I was. That I could be read like a book. That I had to be browbeaten into cleaning my room. That I was a sore trial. That I cared for no one but myself and, worse, that I *thought of* no one but myself. That I'd spoiled my dog, Rip, to such an extent he'd turned vicious and knocked a woman off her bike and now had to be chained to his doghouse like a criminal. That I was always overacting.

"Everyone" was Elsie – Auntie Everyone, the aunt who was raising me. She sprayed her opinions about me as casually as she sprayed Raid around the house.

I had a list of Elsie's best qualities, too, and never lost an opportunity to tell her. That she was bossy. That she never talked, she yelled. That she was without understanding. That she was a gossip. That she was two-faced, because she talked behind people's backs. That she was a monotonous, mediocre, humiliating hypocrite. ("A what?") That she was boring. That she was a cold fish.

Now and then a teacher would confirm Elsie's prevailing view of me.

In grade seven, the vice-principal, Mr. Booth, phoned home to say I was too sophisticated for a schoolgirl. What he said was, "Wearing knee socks in January violates the dress code. Girls are supposed to wear ankle socks or nylons to school unless it is snowing. Then they can wear pants underneath their skirts. But it's not snowing now. Marion is wearing knee socks to get attention."

"See?" Elsie said. "What did I tell you? Anything to get attention."

In guidance class the teacher asked us to list our bad qualities, the things about ourselves that needed improvement. Since I'd rejected Elsie's list, I couldn't think of any. The guidance teacher said this proved I was infested with them, like worms. She phoned home. "Marion is too self-satisfied for a thirteen-year-old."

"See?" Elsie said. "Think you're too big for your own britches."

That year I was accused of giving Miss Wylie, the PE teacher, the finger. She was a tall, pale, nervous woman, like a female Ichabod Crane, and she couldn't get our group to take showers. But I hadn't fingered Miss Wylie. During her overwrought bawling out of the class I'd scratched my nose at the wrong moment. No one believed this action was innocent, and there was another phone call home. I got an "Unsatisfactory" for behaviour in PE. So I joined the grass hockey team. It seemed the sensible thing to do, since Miss Wylie was the coach. Next report card I was back to N for normal.

"See?" I told Elsie. "It's no big deal."

Minor things. Actually, most of my school behaviour was N for normal. "Within normal bounds," a statistician might now say. "Smack in the middle of the bell curve." Invisible.

At school, in those days, your personal history stayed personal. "It's none of their bloody business," Elsie would say, turning into an unexpected ally whenever teachers asked probing questions like, "Where is your mother?" "Why do you live with your aunt?"

"Tell them nothing," Elsie instructed. "Or tell them, 'My mother's on a long vacation. I live with my aunt and uncle. My father visits.'"

ELSIE AND ME. WE were like a pair of athletes playing a special kind of domestic dodgeball. Or like dancers performing a weird, love-hate pas de deux in one of Miss Blythe's, my dancing teacher's, recitals. By the time I was thirteen it seemed we didn't know how else to get along. We were constantly fighting. I'd get angry over the dumbest things. If Elsie said, "Drink up your milk," I'd say, "No!" Even though I wanted it. If she asked, "How was school today?" I'd scream, "Terrible!" Even though it wasn't. She'd yell back, "You're nothing but a time bomb." And "You never listen! Why don't you listen?" And "What did I ever do to deserve such trouble?"

It seemed I had forgotten she loved me. Had taken me in when I was five, almost a foundling. Had replaced my mother and taken over the slop and sweet anguish of child rearing.

At thirteen I was endlessly crashing against her. Her energy matched mine. She never wavered, never gave in, never backed down. Never crumbled before my onslaught. She was the wall, the corral. And I was the wild horse, hysterical for ... what?

I didn't know what.

Like any thirteen-year-old, I didn't know what.

TWO

Marion, Billy, Nancy

There was just the one of me. I was my parents' only child. And when I was five, they separated for good. It was, everyone said, "a rocky marriage." Nancy was Australian and Billy was Canadian and they'd met in Auckland, New Zealand, when Billy was first mate on a freighter that travelled between Canada and New Zealand. According to the stories Elsie told, Nancy married Billy because he was an officer and she thought his family had money. "Hah! Was she ever wrong!" Elsie would laugh. "We were ordinary people. We even made our own clothes!"

Nancy and Billy were married in New Zealand in 1946, when Nancy was thirty and Billy was thirty-nine. I was born in Sydney, Australia, a year after that. Billy, at sea at the time of my birth, received the news – dramatically, I thought – by trans-Pacific cable. There's a picture of me as a newborn being held rather gingerly by Nancy's mother, Marion Whitehouse, a woman I would never come to know. My grandmother has short hair done in waves, and she is wearing a checked wool suit. I am wrapped in a white blanket. The caption on the back of the picture reads, "Two Marions." My middle name, Alice, was for Billy's mother in Canada. Neither of my grandfathers was alive at the time.

Nancy, Billy, and I lived together as a family only once, in a large, rented house in Vancouver for six months when I was three. I played in the street there with other kids, all of us on tricycles like some terrible infant motorcycle gang, and celebrated Halloween for the first time. This was something new for an Australian mother. I was given a small bag for trick-or-treating and sent outside without a costume to join an excited group of pirates, witches, and princesses.

"That whole time in Vancouver was a disaster," Elsie would later claim. This was because Nancy cried much of the time. She hated the rain. She missed Australia. And because, it reputedly got back to Elsie, my father and his family were so boring. Not only that, Elsie would hasten to add, Nancy was restless, wanting things she couldn't find in Canada with my father.

I travelled with Nancy to Australia by boat three times during those early years, leaving Billy in Canada like lost luggage. We lived mostly on cruise ships, but also in Fiji and Tasmania, where Nancy had been born and where her mother and brother still lived. And then finally, when I was five, the story goes, my father – and here Elsie would say with relish, "Billy put his foot down" – declared that my travelling days were over. From now on I'd be living in Canada with him.

There was no fuss the night Nancy handed me over. We were in the tiny cabin of a cruise ship that was docked in Vancouver; the boat was the MV *Aorangi*. Nancy was sitting at a small table and I was beside her. And there was a skinny man wearing a felt hat standing in the narrow doorway before us. He was smiling at me. I'd forgotten what

Billy looked like. Nancy pushed me towards him. "Go on," she said. "That's your father."

Soon after I went to live on Vancouver Island with Billy's sister, Elsie, and her second husband, Ernie Sexton, in an area outside of Victoria known as Cordova Bay. Billy couldn't look after me because he worked on docks up and down the West Coast supervising the loading of lumber; he'd "come ashore" the previous year. But from that time until I was eighteen years old, he visited every other weekend. He never remarried, and, to my knowledge, was never involved with another woman; once was enough.

THREE

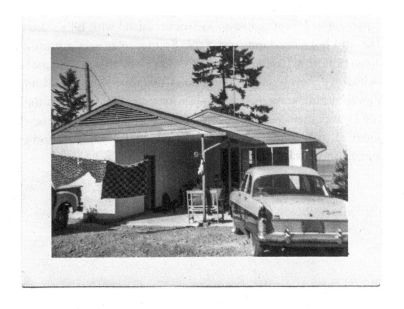

Cordova Bay house

In June of 1960, two months after my thirteenth birthday, a parcel arrived from Nancy in Australia. It was there on the kitchen table when I got home from school.

Elsie was baking at the kitchen counter, making pastry for the meat pie we'd be having for supper. Her arms were covered in flour and she was grinning. "Look what came for you!" She sounded amazed.

I was amazed, too. We hadn't heard from Nancy for, what? Two years?

"It came right out of nowhere," Elsie said with awe. "When I opened the mailbox I was so surprised."

It was a soft, square parcel, and it was sitting innocently enough in the centre of the Arborite table. Yet I hesitated approaching it. It seemed strange being there, at startling odds with the benign and familiar surroundings, like some science-fictiony *thing* from another world, which, once undone, would begin its malevolent work. Days earlier I'd watched *Invasion of the Body Snatchers* on TV: *It all started out innocently enough. No one expected the tiny pods that suddenly appeared to turn into vicious killers* ... In the movie, the one scientist who knows the truth tries uselessly to warn everyone about the pods, hollering in alarm, "Don't touch them! Destroy them immediately!"

This is exactly what I was feeling when I looked at the parcel – alarm, dismay, foreboding. *Invasion of the Body Snatchers* had an eerie lesson, and it was this: anywhere, and at any time, the most ordinary-looking things can turn out to be *something else,* something horrible and merciless that will ultimately drain the life from you. Like alien pods. Or parcels from Australia.

"What's the matter?" Elsie asked, impatient. "Go on, open it up. Looks like she's finally remembered your birthday."

Still I hesitated; I had become used to – even comfortable with – being forgotten by Nancy. I hadn't expected this. You hurry home from school on a sunny afternoon thinking only of your waiting dog and a peanut-butter sandwich and, perhaps, a swim down at the beach. Mindlessly happy is what you are, oblivious of danger. Your returned social studies test with the large red *A* is clasped in your eager hand, a top mark, and you're proud and excited – can't wait! – to show everyone, gloat, bask in the praise you know will be coming as surely as you know the sky is blue. But what happens? There's an unexpected parcel on the kitchen table from a mother you haven't seen in eight years. And suddenly your world threatens to become *Invasion of the Body Snatchers,* with all the predictable and grisly components.

"I'm scared to," I said, glancing at Elsie.

"Scared?" she hooted. "Scared of the parcel?"

"It could be radioactive."

"What?"

"Radioactive. There could be lethal pods inside for ..."

"Oh, for heaven's sake! It's that horror movie you've been watching, isn't it? Well, stop it. This instant. Don't be so ridiculous. You're letting your imagination run away with you. Like you always do."

"But ..."

"But nothing. Open up the bloody thing." I glared at her. "Go on."

I was acting an early scene from the movie when I finally approached the table. I was the trembling, beloved, virginal, beautiful daughter of the hero scientist, about to unleash God knows what.

"If you don't hurry up and open it, I will," Elsie said irritably.

"Okay, okay!"

The parcel was dotted with Australian stamps that had pictures of kangaroos on them, and the brown wrapping paper bore Nancy's strange style of handwriting: all her *M*'s looked like *W*'s. So the address, instead of reading "Miss Marion Gibson," read "Wiss Warion Gibson."

"Go on," Elsie insisted, again. "It won't bite."

There was no help for it: I opened the parcel. Elsie watched my every move. First I undid the knots in the thick string and removed the outer wrapping. Inside was a present wrapped in pink tissue paper, and there was a card attached. No envelope, just a card with a koala bear on the front and writing that said, "Greetings from Down Under." Inside Nancy had written, "Happy Birthday to Warion, Love frow Wother." There was a PS: "One day you'll get a nice surprise."

Tearing off the tissue paper, I pulled out a long, purple, see-through nightgown that was slit up the front and had black feathers – something Elsie called marabou – attached to the plunging neckline. It was a nightgown like the one my cousin Doreen had worn for her wedding night, a negligee. I screwed up my face and held it at arm's length as if it were something smelly. When I did this, another present, unwrapped, dropped out. A pair of red bikini underpants lay on the turquoise tiled floor. Across the bum, stitched in blue, were the words, "Hi Sexy!"

"What on earth?" Elsie shrieked.

I jumped back from the underpants as if they were something alive, a rat, or a huge red maggot, the kind of thing you'd need a long stick or protective clothing to handle.

"Well, I never!" Elsie said, coming closer, peering at the thing on the floor.

Suddenly I felt like crying. But I wasn't sad. I was hot, angry. Because (1) it was a boring and useless present meant for a grown-up woman. And (2) my mother didn't know how old I was. But I wasn't going to show I cared. "It's another stupid present from Nancy," I said dismissively. "Like that stupid koala bear book and that stupid wooden bowl from Tasmania."

But Elsie had gone deaf to me and was shaking her head and laughing, little hiccupping laughs, little guileless tickle-your-fancy kind of laughs. She had the underpants in her hand and was holding them up to the light; they were transparent, like the negligee, and the light shone through them warmly onto her hand and cheek. It made me think of stained-glass windows in a church.

Elsie said, "That Nancy. This really takes the cake. She finally remembers your birthday and she sends something like this. Wait till I tell Maudie!"

"No! Don't tell!" I cried. Because I knew it wouldn't only be Maudie, my other aunt. It would be Ernie, my uncle; Grandma; Elsie's daughters, Doreen and Shirley; Rae-Ella, the hairdresser; Mrs. Holt next door; everyone else in the family; neighbours, strangers, even Len the butcher at Four Ways Market; and especially my father, Billy. Elsie couldn't keep quiet about anything.

"Can't we forget about it?" I pleaded. "Can't we throw it in the garbage?"

She sat down at the kitchen table looking defeated. "Oh, Marion," she sighed. "You shouldn't be too hard on your mother. It's just that ... well ... she doesn't know what it's like to raise a daughter. I'm sure she means well."

"Hah!" I snorted. We both knew this was a ridiculous thing to say. "How can sending a birthday present two months late be meaning well? And what about Dad? Was leaving him 'meaning well'? Was it?"

Elsie sighed again and looked bewildered. "I don't know ... It's just when two people don't ..."

The answer always ended like this – at a locked door. *When two people don't...* The next words – *love one another* – were never spoken. The explanation always ended at *don't*. That's as far as I ever got: I had parents, all right, but they were Nancy and Billy. Two people who don't.

I gathered up the nightgown and the underpants and scrunched them into a ball. I didn't know what I was going to do with them. Maybe use them as costumes for one of my plays. Maybe wear them on Halloween to scare babies.

"Here, give me them," Elsie said, extending a flour-covered arm. "I'll put them away." Then her eyes went wide. "Wait a minute! I know what we can do! We'll give the nightgown to Grandma. Can't you picture Grandma sitting at the kitchen table playing solitaire in a purple negligee?"

I knew this was a lame attempt to humour me, knew she was treating me like a four-year-old. But I laughed anyway. Laughed with relief and gratitude. In an instant my anger switched to amusement. It was as if I were a TV and my channels had been changed.

Everyone laughed at Grandma these days. She was eighty-four and had, it was said, "gone funny." She hummed nursery rhymes and spent her days playing solitaire or dominos at the kitchen table, and she could always be counted on to do or say something deliciously odd. She lived in Victoria with Maudie and Maudie's only son, Kenny. Elsie called him "that useless Kenny Pepper." I called him "that gorgeous Kenny Pepper" after the TV wrestler Gorgeous George. They were both blonds. And I knew that siding with Kenny annoyed Elsie.

"*You* could wear the underpants," I now said, to keep the joke going, enjoying the rare camaraderie between us. And because Elsie was short and plump and wore glasses and was fifty-four years old and it was hilarious to picture her with "Hi Sexy!" written on her bum. It would be like seeing the underpants on miserable old Mrs. Smith, who ran Smith's store, or on Miss Horel, my bossy home ec teacher.

"Hah! Wouldn't that give Ernie a thrill?" Elsie said.

But I recoiled from laughing about *that*. I hadn't thought about *that*. Picturing my pudgy, bald-headed uncle in his beige janitor's clothes getting a thrill out of Elsie in the "Hi Sexy!" underpants was too strange. And why would he love it if she wore the bikini, I wondered?

They didn't sleep in the same bed; they didn't even sleep in the same room. Ernie had been sleeping on the pullout downstairs since last Christmas. The reason for this was still a mystery to me, but ever since, things between them had been horrible. Elsie said Ernie slept downstairs because he snored. "Snore?" Ernie said. "You should listen to yourself!"

The only things Ernie loved that I knew about – other than snore-free sleeps – were chocolate bars with nuts and hard candies; wrestling matches, *Fun-O-Rama,* and *Gunsmoke* on TV; building things in his workshop beside the carport; and all pets, especially my excitable dog, Rip, a large black-Lab-and-collie cross. No, I decided, the underpants would probably make him cranky, because that's what he was most of the time.

"He's a cranky old fart," Elsie often said of him these days. "Don't pay any attention to him."

Still, Ernie as a "cranky old fart" was something I was used to, as familiar and as ordinary in my life as the yellow bedspread on my bed, as the beach of Cordova Bay. Ernie as a lover of bikini underpants was too unbelievable even to consider.

"I wonder what the 'surprise' means," Elsie said, musing over the card in her hand. "Maybe Nancy's finally struck it rich."

"A nice surprise," I said, sarcastically. Sarcasm was something I'd recently discovered and I used it constantly. "Sounds like 'The Teddy Bears' Picnic': 'If you go down in the woods today, you're sure of a big surprise. "The Teddy Bears' Picnic" had been my favourite song when I was five years old; Billy had bought me the record. "And it's not a real birthday card," I added. "It's some old thing she had lying around. Probably that nightgown was an old thing, too."

Elsie agreed, but she was less contemptuous, more thoughtful. "Nancy always did go in for ritzy clothes. This must have cost a pretty penny." She was examining the marabou on the negligee. "It's sewn right into the seam!" she now cried.

I was disgusted. Some present. I searched for words to describe it. "Cruddy." "Putrid." "Absurd." To my annoyance, though, these words kept colliding with "ritzy," a word that sparkled with classiness and allure.

FOUR

Nancy and friends

"My mother," I liked to joke to my friends, "she's missing *and* in action."

By the time I was thirteen she was on her fourth or fifth marriage, maybe even her seventh or eighth, I'd wildly boast. In truth, we never knew for sure how many marriages Nancy had had. But we believed it was a lot, certainly more than the sturdy homemakers of Vancouver Island ever had. As many, I liked to believe, as the movie stars in *Silver Screen* or *Photoplay* magazines – Elizabeth Taylor, Debbie Reynolds, or

Elsie's favourite, Lana Turner. I imagined Nancy, like them, hopscotching from one man to another in a peculiar game of collecting broken hearts. Her quest, as I knew, was to become fabulously rich. "And she doesn't care how she does it," Elsie would usually add.

Each time I told the story of my mother I would exaggerate her stature. My friends heard about a woman of mythological proportions, one who was travelling the world on luxury cruise ships, who dressed like a movie star in gowns and furs, who was dazzlingly beautiful, slim, and dark-haired, who was the life of every party, always laughing from the centre of a ring of admirers, a cigarette holder poised between fingernails painted a vivid Chinese red. Not only that, I'd tell my audience, my mother played the piano so well she could have been a concert pianist if she'd wanted to. She was so *extravagant,* I'd say, using a newly discovered word, that she sent me madcap gifts like purple negligees and "Hi Sexy!" underpants, and once a pair of black-velvet shoes three sizes too big. And when she wasn't travelling the world, I'd add as final evidence of her grandeur, she lived in Australia, that bright, exotic place at the other end of the world.

I'd say, "I was born there, you know."

I'd say, "Australia's like a beautiful desert island, only better."

I loved it when people's mouths fell open. "Oh my, Australia! Lucky you!" And didn't that make me exotic? Wasn't I someone special? And different? And envied?

In this way I paved over Nancy's absence.

There was a picture that summed her up for me then. She's leaning casually on the railing of a cruise ship, a cigarette in a holder dangling from between her fingers. She's young-looking, glamorous. Dressed to the hilt – a fox fur collar around her neck, flower in her hair. But the thing that always grabbed me about this picture was the people beside her. A man and woman to her right, a woman to her left. One woman is wearing a sweater, the other a blouse, and they're without makeup; the man wears an ordinary white shirt. And they're so dowdy, so plain beside Nancy, like three weeds clustered around a rose.

It's not a picture that was given to me but one I found in Maudie's, my other aunt's, photo album. From the stamp on the back of the picture I knew that it had been taken in New Zealand. From Elsie I knew that the coat with the fox fur collar was light blue.

"The Story of the Blue Coat" goes with "The Story of Nancy's First Visit." Elsie's stories. Told many times during my childhood.

I'll never forget that coat of Nancy's. She had it on the first time I ever saw her. A long blue coat with a silver fox fur around the neck. Very sophisticated. I thought, "This can't be my brother's wife." Because she was too grand for him, too swish-looking. And Billy was such a mouse, such a quiet guy.

That day was the first time we saw you, too. A baby, six months old. There'd been a picture of you and Nancy in the Vancouver paper and a write-up saying how you were the first baby to ever fly across the equator, and how Nancy had never seen snow. We saw the article before we ever laid eyes on the pair of you; Billy had sent over a copy. "Mrs. Gibson, wife of Captain W.D. Gibson, and baby Marion arrive in Canada from Australia and see snow for the first time." That's what the article said. Something like that.

But when Billy brought you both to the Island, Nancy took us by surprise. She was so loud, so forward. It was like some fancy bird had landed in my kitchen. She plunked herself down on a kitchen chair and right away said, "Well, where's the cocktails?" Cocktails! In the middle of the afternoon! She made everybody shy. We were such a drab bunch compared to her.

But the thing I noticed that day was the way Billy did all the looking after you. Feeding you, changing your diaper. Nancy couldn't have cared less. She was more interested in getting Ernie to fix her cigarette lighter, which had broke. Or showing off her clothes to my girls. Her blue coat and her fox fur. And her shoes! She had plastic high heels with dice floating in some liquid in the heels. No one had ever seen anything like it. The girls couldn't get over them. They thought Nancy was a movie star.

But for me there was no fun in looking at Nancy's clothes. She made me jealous. Beside her I felt so poor and ordinary. And when she started making up to Ernie, flirting with him, I didn't know what to do. Later I learned what she was like. She'd make up to any man. Just for the fun of it. Just to see the other woman squirm.

The story always made *me* squirm when I heard it. Nancy "lolling about," as Elsie called it, with her cigarette lighter and her plastic high-heeled shoes, demanding cocktails while Billy changed my diaper. I liked hearing about Billy's part in the story, though, that he was the one looking after me.

FIVE

Billy at sea

It was understood that Nancy had broken Billy's heart. It was also understood that we were never to mention her name within his hearing. That would be a cruel thing to do and might cause his heart to break again.

Billy lived in a bachelor suite in Vancouver. When I was younger I thought he kept his broken heart at the back of his dresser drawer and only took it out on Friday afternoons to glue back together before his trip to the Island. I imagined then that his heart was like an egg that had cracked open when Nancy left us for the last time. I also believed that when your heart broke you cried your eyes out. There you were, alone with the pieces of your broken heart, and with no eyeballs either, utterly miserable on your tear-soaked bed. It was the worst thing that could happen to a person. And it had happened to Billy.

Once when I was being difficult with him – I was eight or nine – Elsie pulled me aside and hissed, "You be nice to your daddy. You're all he has."

Meaning: Don't *you* break his heart as well. Don't you be like your mother.

Still, I wanted to know: How had Nancy done this terrible thing? How did she break Billy's heart?

"By being selfish and thinking of no one but herself," Elsie would say. Then add, almost as an afterthought, "And that time in Vancouver. Running off for two weeks with an officer from Billy's ship ..."

"Yes, but his heart. Why did it break?" I pressed, not wanting to believe that such an important thing as a heart could be so easily damaged.

"He didn't have his head screwed on," Elsie said. "He was head over heels."

BILLY WAS A SMALL man, slight in build, and balding, with a fringe of hair that was dark brown, flecked with grey. I thought his eyes were wonderful. They were a special shade of milky-blue, like the colour of the sea and sky when they melt together on a hot summer's afternoon.

There was a cot covered with woollen blankets in the basement of Elsie and Ernie's house for him to sleep on. He'd arrive on a Friday night swinging his leather suitcase – he called it his grip – the same bag he used when he went to sea. Inside it, sometimes, when I was small, there'd be a present for me – a colouring book, a kaleidoscope – though Elsie soon put a stop to that. "You'll spoil her," she told him. "She'll only want to see you for the presents."

Then he'd spend the weekend just with me. He'd do anything I wanted. Go to the park. Movies. Out for chocolate ice creams. Play

Snakes and Ladders. Help me with homework. And when I was younger, watch my plays – re-enactments of Hans Christian Andersen's "The Princess and the Pea," and of "Cinderella" and "Snow White." I was always the star and played every part, specializing in the wicked stepmothers and witches, the brave-but-slighted princesses. Billy was always the audience of one. The audience clapped and clapped and found me delightful! What a delightful little girl!

To my friends I said, "My father's a captain. He has his master's ticket. He can navigate by the stars." I said, "My father comes over from the mainland every other weekend just to see me." I said, "My father's rich; he bought Elsie a car so she can take me to dancing lessons. He can play the banjo, too."

If a grown-up wanted to know about Billy, Elsie had two stories at the ready. The shorter version was for strangers, people met in passing – a woman in a lineup at the wool store, a neighbour's sister, and, once, as I stood mute by her side, in chatty conversation with my grade four teacher, Mrs. Turvey, when it was discovered that in "real life" Mrs. Turvey was a housewife who knit and made her own clothes just as Elsie did. The shorter version about Billy was the exalted one, the one meant to impress and to lay flat any suspicion on the part of the hearer that Elsie's family – she called us Me and Mine – were anything less than exemplary. (It was the same thing I did when I boasted to friends about my absent parents – derailed any criticisms of my unusual family life by declaring it spectacular.) Even while sensing this distortion, the falseness of this public presentation, I still shamelessly loved the warm glances people would give me after Elsie told the story, glances that said, "For goodness' sake, a captain! And he still had time to father this lovely child!" Privately, I called this story "Sailing the Deep Blue Sea." It was as brief and as soothing to my ears as a lullaby, and it began:

My brother, Marion's father. Now there's a hard worker. He started out as a cabin boy, you know, and worked his way up the ladder, all the way to deep-sea captain. And look at him now! In charge of the Vancouver waterfront!

Then there was the other story, the one hauled out for family and friends. This story, it was understood, was the real one, the plain, cold truth, the one without the varnish, as frank and everyday as a filet of sole set out on the counter for frying, as the ratty elastic bandages Grandma wore on her swollen legs, as Ernie's old blue truck with the rusty back fender. I called it "Sad Billy" because of the way it made me feel, and because it seemed to go with my own story about his broken heart. The way Elsie told this story, you'd think Billy's life was over.

He was an unpredictable kid. Everything he did was in a rush. For example, the way he ate his supper. Ma made him count between mouthfuls. Otherwise he'd gulp it down and be finished before anyone else had started. Everything Billy did was too fast. He didn't know what "walk" meant. He ran everywhere and was always covered in cuts and bruises. He'd be running and not looking where he was going. The times he banged into furniture, walls, telephone poles. Because he wasn't watching out.

When he was sixteen he got on the boats. The merchant marines. And that slowed him down. Because he had to follow rules. Pretty soon he was a different person, everything neat and careful. When he'd come home on leave we were surprised at the new way he was eating, cutting up meat with a knife and fork and not shoving it in his mouth with his hand like before.

Other things changed, too. He was a noisy kid, yelling out what he wanted to say, pulling pranks. One time he lit Ma's tablecloth on fire. He was underneath it playing with matches. But after he went on the boats he got quiet. Maybe because he was working hard, studying in his spare time to get his tickets. He went from cabin boy at sixteen to captain by the time he was forty-one.

Before Nancy he was in love with Ruth Parkinson. This was when he was in his late twenties. But Ruth was a very tall girl, and I think Billy felt stupid being with her because he was so short. So they broke it off. He felt inferior because of his height. I don't think Ruth minded him being short but it bothered Billy. He couldn't stand being made fun of. He must have felt awkward walking down the street with her.

Ten years went by before he met Nancy. When that finally broke up he wouldn't talk about it. We never discussed my raising Marion, either. He just left her with me. It was only after Nancy had been gone three years that I said to Billy, "Nancy's not coming back, is she?" and he said, "No." So then I knew I had Marion for good.

Everyone was proud of Billy. For what he'd become. The only one of us to do something important. He was the captain of cargo ships, and when he came ashore, he supervised the docks in Vancouver. But this was a side of him we didn't see very often. His working life. Once in a while I'd get a glimpse when he'd get a phone call at my house, something to do with the loading of ships. And I'd always be amazed at the way his voice changed when he talked to his men. Bossy, loud. He'd be telling some guy what to do. Sounding gruff and important.

About his life in Vancouver, in his apartment, I think he was a hermit. He lived a lonely life, keeping to himself. All his life he wanted a home of his own, but he never got it.

Once, though, Billy did write about having a home – with Nancy. When I was nine and visiting him with Elsie, Ernie, Grandma, and Maudie at his bachelor suite in Vancouver, I discovered his "book" in the walk-in closet. It was in a cardboard box of souvenirs from the South Pacific, shoved beneath a net sack filled with black rocks and shrivelled vanilla beans. There was a pair of carved heads in the box, too, a Fijian man and woman made of shiny, brown wood. Billy and the rest of the family were busy getting tea; for the moment I wasn't missed. I settled on the floor to read, but my heart was pounding, the way it did when I snooped in Elsie's or Maudie's dresser drawers – trespassing, looking for secrets.

Billy's story was set in Fiji. The "book" was actually a postcard pamphlet about the Islands, only seven pages long. He'd scratched out the title on the inside cover – *The Fiji Islands* – and printed above it, "Magnetic Island" and "Dear Nancy." There were fourteen colour pictures in the book, reproduced paintings of palm trees, beaches, sunsets, thatched huts – and above and below each picture Billy had created a story about himself and Nancy. I read fast and hungrily.

Page 1: A picture of a cove. Palm trees. A pink-and-blue sunset. This pearl that nestled so peacefully in the broad Pacific. Majestically superb in its natural simplicity. We knew then we had found our paradise. It was here we decided to make our home.

Page 3: A picture of three boys standing on a beach. Palm trees in the distance. The same pink-and-blue sky. Another tribute to the charm of a gracious lady. How fortunate I am! This was the beginning of a bond, children would later strengthen it.

I found myself crying. Elsie called my name. Still I read.

Page 5: Another lagoon seen through the trunks of palm trees. The sky, peach coloured. It was a peculiar day when you took this photo, for we were both sad and happy. Sad because on the morrow we were leaving our island, happy because yet another dream was about to be fulfilled. Soon there would be three of us. There were tears in our eyes ...

Elsie called my name again. Wiping my eyes, I hurriedly put everything away. Just in time.

"What are you doing in here?"

"Nothing."

But I'd found the evidence of my father's broken heart.

SIX

TV set and neighbour's cat

$\mathcal{N}ot$ *long after the purple negligee arrived, Elsie* said, "You should write and thank your mother for the present."

It was before supper, and I was sprawled on the couch in the tiny room at the front of the house that Elsie and Ernie called the den. I was watching *Fun-O-Rama* with Ernie. The toothpaste commercial was on – "Brusha, brusha, brusha. Get the new Ipana." Which meant *The Three Stooges* would be next. I didn't want to be bothered writing a letter.

"Why?" I muttered under my breath.

Ernie heard and looked up and smirked. I stared at him, trying to make my eyes burn into the top of his head. The gesture was supposed to mean "shut up." He'd have been told about the horrible negligee by now. But who knew what he was thinking? He hardly ever spoke. "Like his father," Elsie often complained. "Just sits there with his mouth shut. Never says two words."

Elsie leaned against the doorway with a lit cigarette in her hand. "Did you hear me?" she said, sounding irritated. "You should write a thank-you note to your mother. It's the proper thing to do."

The Three Stooges theme song came on: "Hickory, Dickory, Dock."

"Not now," I answered.

Already Ernie was squirming in his chair, grinning in anticipation; he loved *The Three Stooges*. He had a cigarette burning in the ashtray on the side table, and he reached for it without taking his eyes off the TV. *The Three Stooges* was our favourite *Fun-O-Rama* show. Our next favourites were *Popeye* and *Mighty Mouse* cartoons.

"Marion! Did you hear me?"

"Yes. All right. Leave me alone. I'm watching TV."

The "Malice in the Palace" episode was on, the one where Curly, Larry, and Moe are waiters and keep dumping trays of food over everyone's heads. Ernie and I had watched it a ton of times. I always thought it was funny that people in the shows called the Stooges boys. They were at least as old as Ernie, and Curly even looked like him.

Elsie was still standing there. "Well?" she demanded.

"Well what?"

"The letter."

"After supper."

"Shush!" Ernie said loudly. He was mad because of the interruption. His face was red. He had large lips, fish lips I secretly called them, and he had a habit of licking them, so that his lips were always shiny, purply-red.

"Oh, for goodness' sake," Elsie said. "A grown man watching that junk. Sometimes I wonder what I've married."

Ernie ignored her. Moe had just stuck two fingers into Larry's eyes.

AFTER SUPPER I SPENT ten minutes with a piece of paper torn from my English notebook and wrote:

Dear Wother,

Thank you for the present. It's nice. Purple is an interesting colour. I'w fine. Hom are you? I just had wy thirteenth birthday. Suwwer holidays start in tmo meeks.

Frow Warion

This was my first piece of written satire. I was thrilled with it. I'd never experienced such pleasure writing anything for school. I continued with the return address:

WISS WARION GIBSON
4921 Cordova Bay Rd.
Saanich Peninsula
Vancouver Island
Victoria, B.C.
Canada
The Morld

Writing this put Nancy in her place – far away – and made her seem hilariously incompetent, someone who couldn't even form her *M*'s and *W*'s properly. Writing this put me securely in my place.

At thirteen, everyone said I was a smarty-pants. A smart aleck. A wiseacre. A pain in the ass.

I thought I was a barrel of laughs.

SEVEN

Ernie, Elsie, Grandma

Cordova Bay was a semirural area of farms and seaside houses five miles outside of Victoria. Billy's family claimed lineage to Cordova Bay dating back to the 1920s, when for a few brief but extravagant years his parents had owned a summer place there. My grandfather was a barber, but also a drinker and a gambler, and he'd won the tiny plot of land in a card game. It was flat and treeless, about the size of a baseball diamond, not waterfront, but a short walk from the northern end of the beach. For several summers his family and assorted relatives tented on the property. But in another card game my grandfather lost the property, and summers at Cordova Bay came to a humiliating end.

Then, in the early 1950s, Elsie and Ernie bought a narrow waterfront lot at the south end of Cordova Bay from Old Man Head, a frail neighbour of theirs in Victoria, and it was as if the family had been restored to its rightful place in the world. There was a sense of prestige regained, of wrongs made right; the family was "back out the Bay."

In an attempt to make the new house fit the lot, Ernie had built it like a train, in a series of small stuccoed boxes, with each box – den, bedrooms, bathroom, kitchen, living room – attaching itself to the next one until they reached the rocky bit of land overlooking the beach. The house had turquoise trim and a long gravel driveway.

This was the house where I'd lived with Elsie and Ernie since I was five years old, and the house where Billy visited. Now that I was set down in a place I trusted as permanent, I held fast. Like a barnacle, I told myself, relishing the image of immovability.

The Bay, as we called it, stretched beyond the shore for miles across to D'Arcy Island, an island that had once been a leper colony. Closer in, there was Seal Rock, which you could wade to on the lowest tides, when the double sandbar reached it like a shimmering bridge. There was the gentle curve of the mile-long beach with its fine sand and pebbles and scattered driftwood logs bleached by the sun. Pampas grass grew like a boundary between the beach and the places where the summer cottages began. On hot summer afternoons, agitated sand flies skimmed the sand's surface. I'd watch hundreds of them feeding on the rotting seaweed that was strewn, half-hidden, like beige rags in the sand; you could kick at patches of it and watch the flies swoop off together like a flock of startled birds. The sharp iodine smell of seaweed was a marvellous thing, pungent and rank; thick beds of seaweed floated near the shore at high tide, looking like the long green hair of mermaids. And always there were seagulls cruising over the water's surface, and farther out, sailboats silently drifting.

The Point at the southern end of Cordova Bay was a special place for my friends and me. We gathered there between swims in summer, or met there during winter when the water was swollen-looking from rain or cold blue and choppy during a storm. The Point marked the place where the sandbar ended and the beach turned into cliffs. We claimed it as our own.

Standing at the top of the bank behind our house, eager to be running free with Rip on the sandbar below, I'd often feel exhilarated. By the light, and the brightness, and by the sense of endless space. The sea and sky on a still summer's day looked like a watercolour created with two or three strokes of the brush.

I'd be standing there, my breath catching in my throat.

EIGHT

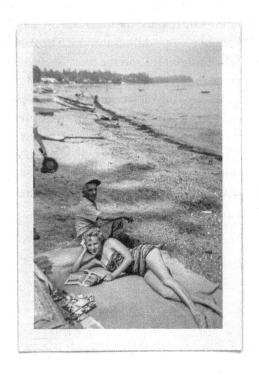

Doreen and Billy

Within days, both family and neighbours knew about my mother's present. It had become "The Story of the Purple Negligee." It was mainly Elsie's story, because she did most of the telling. "Laugh? I thought I'd die!" she said repeatedly about the moment the negligee was revealed. To Mrs. Holt next door. On the phone to Ernie's sister Mildred. To her daughter Doreen, my married cousin.

Long-distance to Shirley, her other married daughter, in California. More than once to Maudie.

The purple negligee and the "Hi Sexy!" underpants had become another family event, as was anything concerning Nancy. I should have known it was useless to plead for privacy. Yet I no longer felt bothered by the gift. Surprisingly, transforming it into a story drained it of any power it had to upset me. And I liked the notoriety the story gave me, liked that it centred on me, that because of me there was a story. Elsie could tell it as much as she wanted. I was content to hang around the edges like a movie director, smugly observing how everyone played their part, delighting in their mock outrage on my behalf, the easy laughs. I liked hearing about myself in the third person; it was like watching yourself on TV.

"Laugh? I thought I'd die!" I now told my friends. "I've sure got one crazy mother."

DOREEN, ALONG WITH HER husband, Bob, and her year-old baby, Lyn, drove out to the Bay with Maudie and Grandma to have a look at my birthday gift. The family did everything together, always. They moved through life in a posse – Sunday dinners, summer vacations, daily visits or telephone calls. No one seemed to have a life of their own, a private life; it was all family. Solitude was suspect, something to be pitied and avoided. Wanting to be by yourself was considered antisocial, even morbid. At thirteen I'd often refuse to go along on Sunday drives, dreading another dull afternoon wedged between Grandma and Maudie in the back seat of Billy's Zephyr. I wanted to read, do anything rather than be imprisoned with my family.

"What?" Elsie would snap. "We're not good enough for you? A book's more interesting than us?"

"Yes," I'd counter, effectively silencing her for at most thirty seconds.

"That's the trouble with you," she'd fluster. "You've got a mind of your own."

There were no books in the house, not proper ones. Only *TV Guide*, magazines filled with knitting patterns, the medical encyclopedia hidden away in the basement pantry. The only real books were my own few: schoolbooks, library books about girl ballerinas, collections of fairy tales – Hans Christian Andersen, the Brothers Grimm – and the two Mark Twain titles that Billy had given me for my thirteenth birthday.

"Why don't you ever read a book?" I'd challenge while Elsie and Ernie watched *Gunsmoke* or *The Ed Sullivan Show*, thinking, "They're as stupid as slugs." If I had a mind of my own, they shared theirs with half a dozen people.

Elsie: "We're not bookish people."

Ernie: "I work at the library. I spend all day surrounded by books. You think I want to look at books on my time off?"

The gifts from Nancy were placed on the empty kitchen table like exhibits at a criminal trial. Laughing, "Oh, Marion!" Doreen was the first to snatch up the negligee. At twenty-seven, she was the elder of Elsie's daughters, and I thought of her as my sister. She had short, white-blond hair done in kiss curls around her face and long dancer's legs, and she had been one of the stars in Miss Blythe's dance troupe. I'd cut out and kept the picture of her that had been in the *Victoria Daily Times* when she married. The headline said, "Well-known Dancer Weds." My friend Doris and I would have long discussions about Doreen. How beautiful was she? More beautiful than cute? Definitely. More beautiful than pretty? For sure. Ravishing? Not ravishing, that was too sexy. Famously beautiful, then? Sort of. She'd had her picture in the paper, hadn't she?

Doreen held the negligee in front of her, testing it for size, then waltzed with it around the kitchen, singing, "Heaven, I'm in heaven ..." She twirled and she leaped; she stood on her toes and then did the splits. Finally, she made a deep bow and flung the negligee at Bob, where it landed on his head. Everyone was laughing. She was lovely to watch and funny; she'd turned the negligee into a parody and Nancy into a parody as well. I loved her for it.

"This is way nicer than the one I had for my honeymoon," she said, panting from the performance. "Now I've only got old flannelette nightgowns."

I wanted to give her the negligee. Then she gushed, "Oh, Auntie

Nancy was always such fun. Everything's so dull without her," and I changed my mind. "I miss her," Doreen continued. "Remember how she'd play Auntie Maudie's piano and get everyone singing?"

"That was eight years ago," Elsie said.

"I know. But wasn't she fun?"

"Hah! Fun!" Elsie said. "You don't know the half of it!"

Bob liked the underpants. He was twenty-eight years old and worked in a bank, a tall, skinny, dark-haired guy who liked playing baseball and drinking beer on weekends and who'd been raised on a farm up-Island. He and Doreen had been married for five years by now. Apparently he'd never seen anything like those underpants. He kept staring at them and grinning. "Well, whaddya know?" he said over and over. They made such an impression on him that from then on, "Hi Sexy!" became his standard greeting to me.

When it was Maudie's turn to hold the negligee she said wonderingly, "Isn't it fancy! So sheer. Imagine wearing such a thing."

Doreen and Elsie exchanged looks. Maudie had been a widow for eleven years and was reputed to hate sex. It was not possible to imagine her wearing such a thing. "She did it once and that made Kenny." This was common knowledge via Elsie. "After that – forget it!"

"Imagine washing it," Elsie now said, changing the subject. "That marabou would take forever to dry."

"You wouldn't catch the Queen wearing something like that," Grandma snorted. "It wouldn't be allowed."

We looked at her. Lately, the Queen was all she talked about.

"Hey, Grandma," Bob hollered, because Grandma was deaf. He pointed to the underpants. "What about these? Would the Queen wear these?"

"I'm not deaf," Grandma said, snatching the underpants and shoving them into her purse. It was the last anyone saw of them.

"Laugh? I thought I'd die!" Elsie said again. "When Marion opened up that parcel and ..."

"Pipe down in there!" This from Ernie in the den. Saturday-afternoon wrestling was on. "I can't hear a bloody thing!"

He was watching another grudge match between Gorgeous George and his favourite wrestler, Whipper Billy Watson. Stomping around the ring – the slow-motion moves, the fake agony – I thought wrestlers looked like apes wearing diapers. Snidely, I'd mention this to Ernie, who'd be on the edge of his chair, moving his shoulders and groaning along with the TV figures. He always ignored me. Elsie and Doreen, however, loved the image.

Now Elsie yelled, "What's to hear? It's just a bunch of grunting men," and Doreen screamed with laughter.

"Gorgeous George would look good in the negligee, Pop!" she shouted. "It'd match his gorgeous blond hair."

Everyone laughed.

"Pipe down, for the love of God!" Ernie hollered and turned up the TV. "Is it too much to ask for a little peace and quiet?"

Elsie and Doreen looked at each other with pretend fear and giggled some more.

"Men!" Elsie said dismissively. Until then, Bob had been laughing along with the women. Now he didn't know what to do. So he turned to me and punched me on the shoulder. "Whaddya say, Hi Sexy? Want to throw the ball around?"

We headed outside. But we heard Doreen laughing as we went. "Poor Bob! He didn't know whether to shit or wind his watch."

"None of them ever do," Elsie said.

NINE

Elsie

If 1960 were assigned a colour, it would be turquoise,
not the black-and-white of our TV screens. Nineteen sixty was at the
apex of the turquoise years. The colour dominated our lives like a vast
vinyl cushion; everyone was crazy about it. Turquoise was the only
colour that mattered, a particular shade of blue-green that was bright,
optimistic, and, above all, modern. It transformed everything: houses,

clothes, cars, and, at Easter, even the fur of live rabbits. I'd wanted a turquoise rabbit in the worst way but Elsie had said, "Over my dead body. You wouldn't look after it. I'd have to. And that's all I need. A bloody rabbit."

"A bloody *turquoise* rabbit!" I protested, but it was no use. I had to make do with an Easter basket that had turquoise eggs and turquoise plastic hay.

Plastic was good, too. Anything plastic. In 1960 anything plastic *and* turquoise was the top of the mountain; you couldn't get any higher, any more modern, than that. Elsie had a set of turquoise plastic dishes she kept for special occasions. Doris and I had turquoise rubber thongs.

"Is rubber plastic?" we asked each other, worried.

Ernie was in his workshop banging nails when we consulted him.

"Everything's plastic," he said. "Even my new dentures." He took them out to show us, placing them on the shiny platform of his table saw. A full set of plastic teeth, pink gums and all, just like the real thing.

"Holy," we said, Ernie standing there with a collapsed mouth.

"Holy," we said again.

But ultimately it was turquoise that got our vote. You could colour everything with it – metal, wood, concrete. I was proud that our house was awash in it, because this told the world that we were right up there alongside everyone else. Even if our house was little and built like a train, even if Ernie was a janitor and wore work clothes instead of a suit and tie when he went off to work each dark morning, we could hold our heads up. As a colour, turquoise was truly democratic; it made us as good as everyone else. Even as good as the Holts next door, who stubbornly went in for brown clothes and pink house trim.

"Must be because they're from England and old-fashioned," I told Doris. How else to account for such a glaring lack of style?

Without question Elsie was the queen of turquoise. Whatever she said, went; the rest of us fell in line, especially Ernie, whose around-the-house work pants were splattered with turquoise paint. Elsie was the colourist and the designer of our lives, and she never hesitated. She knew exactly what she wanted, and it was turquoise *everything*.

The floor tiles in our kitchen and bathroom were turquoise, and so were the stove and fridge, the bathtub and toilet. The trim on the house was turquoise; the throw cushions in the den were turquoise; the full porcelain skirt of the figurine Elsie kept on top of the TV in the den was turquoise. Hand soap came in white, pink, and turquoise; we had them all, but the turquoise bars went first. Elsie had made herself a turquoise shorty coat for driving in the car, and me, turquoise pedal-pushers as well as shorts with a matching sleeveless top trimmed in white rickrack, my official summer outfit. Ernie and Billy had received identical home-knit turquoise cardigans from Elsie the previous Christmas; they'd worn them like twins, or a brave-but-diminished team, to watch *Hockey Night in Canada* on the first and third Saturday nights of the month, when Billy was over. Elsie sewed a giant-size turquoise-and-yellow terry cloth beach towel for me so I wouldn't keep running off with the bathroom towels, also turquoise. The whole world was in on it, even my dentist, Dr. Middleton. After my last filling he'd acted like a magician and pulled a turquoise plastic toothbrush from behind his back and bowed.

In 1960, turquoise was the colour that was leading us into the happy future. We felt confident and hopeful striding beneath our dazzling turquoise banners. If we could have changed the stripes on the old Canadian flag, the Union Jack, from red and blue to red and turquoise, we would have done that, too.

IN THE SPRING OF 1960 several important things were going on in the world. The Soviet Union was preparing to launch the first planetary probe to Mars; one hundred and fifty thousand people rioted in the streets of Tokyo over the US pact with Japan; D.H. Lawrence's *Lady Chatterley's Lover* was still banned in Canada as obscene; and France detonated a nuclear bomb.

My family couldn't have cared less.

Actually, most people couldn't have cared less. Teachers. Friends' parents. Neighbours. Nobody that I knew talked about these things. World events was a dull, ten-minute segment in my social studies class. And even then it was about past world events like WW II (most of the men teachers were ex-military) or the discovery of the polio vaccine; the events were never current.

But something called The Red Menace did get a passing, though superficial, hold on people's attention that spring. Initially this rather vague threat involved ludicrous-looking communists with shaved heads wearing ill-fitting suits, and spies, and "The Cold War," which I imagined took place across the frozen expanse of Siberia. Then something specific happened: a US spy plane piloted by Francis Gary Powers was shot down over the Soviet Union, and everyone started actively worrying about the "Reds," the "Communist Hordes" who might invade the "Free World," meaning Canada and the United States. This event was treated like a new but scary TV show. We'd watch grainy black-and-white footage of planes droning through empty skies and army tanks hurrying across open stretches of land. We'd watch while solemn and well-dressed men, the TV announcers, told us what President Eisenhower had said and what the Soviets were threatening. Outside our windows the sun shone so beneficently it was strange to consider there was such a thing as peril in the world. Who could figure it? It didn't seem real.

Still, a fleeting mood of alarm gathered, and my aunt and uncle, for that brief time, became quiet and tight-lipped. Billy, on his weekend visit, tolled the funeral bell when he said grimly, "It's World War Three. Mark my words."

But he was wrong. The Red Menace soon passed as a major news event, dropped like a TV show nobody wanted to watch. We went back to comfy local stories like the one about the new ferry being launched from the Island to Vancouver; the *Daily Times* said that passengers complained it was too fast. And the news about the big Mayfair Mall being built downtown.

Elsie announced with relief, "Well, now we can get back to normal." As though she'd endured a brief bit of chaos – a snowstorm, say, with puddles of mud and snow on her kitchen floor – but had everything cleaned up now.

Elsie's usual reaction to the distressing things going on in the wider world was to shiver with annoyance. "Turn the bloody thing off," she'd order Ernie or me whenever the TV news was most bleak – murders, wars. "I've got better things to do than get morbid over that bloody stuff."

"Better things to do" stood for the smooth daily and weekly – and yearly – round of keeping house: sewing, knitting, cooking, and cleaning.

The latter was a thing she apparently loved. "Some days I'd rather scrub a wall than have a conversation," she'd say. It was an enthusiasm I never did learn to share. Then there was grocery shopping at Four Ways Market in Victoria, visiting Maudie and Grandma, and having her hair done by Rae-Ella. It was all so achingly dull, I thought, one gigantic yawn.

Elsie stayed home and kept house like most women did. The only other options were nurse, teacher, or secretary, or, like the absent Nancy, breaker of men's hearts. Dripping disdain, I intended to reject all of these options. I was going to be an Explorer, or a Kennel Owner, or change my name to Liza Lane and produce and star in Broadway musicals. I hadn't decided which. But I was definitely not going to get married and "keep house." What a stupid thing to do! As far as I could tell, the house kept you. Every woman I knew was a borderline maniac who viewed her home as a luxury hotel for germs and disease-bearing insects. At our house I was constantly gagging on bleach fumes. Raid was sprayed everywhere like air freshener; we often ate dinner beneath a cloud of it. In fact, Elsie bought Raid by the case lot. She stacked the red-and-yellow cans in the basement pantry beside her canned beans and raspberries and jars of blackberry jam.

"I'm never getting married," I announced peevishly that spring over a supper of meat loaf and baked potatoes. "I'm never going to be trapped in a house with puking babies and have to wash clothes and scrub floors and make supper for everyone like a slave. It's disgusting!"

Elsie paused, a homemade pickled beet on her fork, and looked at me levelly. "That's what they all say," she smirked.

"NORMAL" FOR ERNIE WAS getting up at five every weekday morning. He was the janitor at the Victoria Public Library, arriving there by six to start the heating system, three boilers hidden away like a murky secret in the library basement. The boilers were huge and round and made of steel; they had metal ladders attached to their sides, like ominous-looking spaceships. They sounded dangerous, too, hissing away with their dials and steam valves. I was always nervous visiting Ernie in his boiler room at the library. Any minute, I believed, the boilers might explode, and we – Ernie and me and the librarians toiling quietly above us – would be fatally scalded, dying horribly amid a mountain of hot wet books.

Ernie was so conscientious about his job that he'd once walked to work in a snowstorm to open the library on time when he couldn't get his truck out of the driveway.

"A martyr, that's what he is" was Elsie's comment. "What's the matter with closing the library for a day? No one gives a damn about books when it's snowing."

I pictured him trudging head down through the storm with his tin lunch bucket clutched to his chest. Inside: bologna sandwiches, brownies, and a thermos of sustaining tea. A hero! Victoria readers should have awarded him a plaque; the mayor should have shaken his hand. But what happened? At the three-mile point, the police picked him up and drove him the rest of the way in. Victoria book lovers never knew how lucky they were. "My uncle practically runs the library," I'd tell my friends in my usual boastful way. "If it wasn't for him, there wouldn't *be* a library!"

Ernie's working day ended at two in the afternoon. By three he'd be asleep on the pullout downstairs. And at four he'd be in his brown recliner in front of the TV watching *Fun-O-Rama*. When he wasn't watching TV, he was working in his "shop," a pokey room off the carport that contained the table saw and a wall of wrenches, hammers, and jars of nails. Ernie always seemed old to me, though when I was thirteen I knew him to be fifty-three, a year younger than Elsie and the same age as my father.

I thought Elsie treated Ernie like dirt. She was so snappy and bossy with him, always telling him to fix something or build something – an elaborate brick barbecue, a coffee table, a rock wall for a flowerbed, a special bench for her sewing. Usually he'd say, "Nag, nag," under his breath but loud enough to be heard, before going off and doing what he was told.

Now and then I'd try acting like Elsie and order him to do something, sounding to myself like one of the ugly stepsisters in *Cinderella*: "Ernie, fix my bike!" "Ernie, pick me up from school!"

Usually he'd look right through me as if he hadn't heard. Sometimes, though, he'd sadly shake his head so that I'd feel ashamed of the way I'd treated him and want to make it up. "Let's see what's on TV!" I'd say with false excitement if he wasn't already watching it. Or, "Need any help in the shop?" And he always did. I spent a lot of time holding the measuring tape for him while he measured planks for bookcases (a library job he had on the side) or sweeping up hills of sawdust and shovelling it into pails to lug to the incinerator at the side of the house. In this way I became accidentally but deeply familiar with the surfaces of planks and two-by-fours and with the smell of sawed wood, varnish, and carpenter's glue.

Occasionally Ernie would speak to me sharply. "Turn off the light. You think I work for the BC Electric?" "Don't park your bike on the front steps. No one can get in the bloody door." If I called him when he was outside or in his shop, and he was in a good mood, he'd answer, "Whaaaat-eeee" in two long, drawn-out notes like a song. Then I knew I could ask him for a ride somewhere or a quarter for Smith's store. Once I was eating Planters peanuts while we watched *Fun-O-Rama*. Ernie looked over at me and scowled. "You shouldn't be eating those things," he said. "They don't get digested. They come out whole in your turds."

"You eat peanuts," I said, affronted, mainly by his use of the word "turd." "There's peanuts in your chocolate bars."

"Not the same thing," Ernie said seriously. "They're a different kind of nut. They dissolve."

He broke off a piece of the chocolate bar he was eating – Cadbury Dairy Milk with Nuts – and handed it to me. "Here, this is better for you than those things," he said, glowering at the offending bag.

I sucked away on the chocolate, bits of nut scraping the inside of my mouth. "Whole peanuts tear up your insides," Ernie said, turning back to the TV. "Makes a terrible mess. From getting stuck in your turds. And don't you forget it."

"No," I said. "I won't."

[TEN]

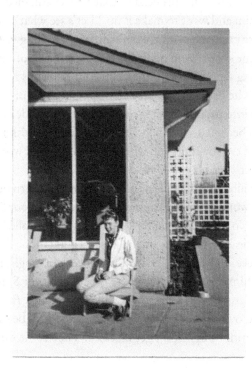

Doris Jones

Doris Jones, my best friend that spring and summer, was a lanky girl with short, curly red hair and a smattering of freckles across her nose and cheeks. Like me Doris didn't want to grow up. We hated the idea of breasts. Breasts were a betrayal. Of childhood, of freedom. It was much grander to remain heedless and without responsibility – to play endlessly on the beach, to build tree forts.

Or to put on a song-and-dance review for the neighbourhood, calling it *Bon Voyage*, the way we'd done two summers earlier. That was the first time one of my "plays" had moved out of my bedroom and into larger life; I was both the director and one of the show's stars, experiencing the excitement of mounting the production, of having a cast of neighbourhood kids to boss around and a ready audience of parents and neighbours to eventually watch the show. We did skits and dance numbers that travelled through different countries – Switzerland, Japan, France – and even back through time, to the 1920s. We rehearsed all summer, painted scenery, sold blackberries by the side of the road to buy the records we needed for the musical numbers, and made tickets using sheets of carbon paper Ernie brought home from the library: *Bon Voyage!! A Musical Extravaganza!! Only 25 Cents!! On Kirkendales' Back Deck!! Starring ...*

The following summer, in a rush of enthusiasm, Doris and I had tried to make clam chowder on the beach, running to Elsie and to Doris's mother for carrots, a potato, an onion. We tossed freshly dug clams into Elsie's old enamel canning pot and hastily gathered branches from overhanging poplars, green wood for a beach fire that refused to stay lit. Several more hurried climbs were made up the cliff through the rough salal, for salt and fresh water. Eventually we grew hot and bored and, laughing, kicked the soup pot over and threw ourselves into the ocean, clothes and all.

We wanted to stay free like that, with everything and nothing to do. Even though breasts had begun for both of us. I had grown three inches since Christmas and was now long-legged and long-armed, like a gorilla, I thought. I was taller than Elsie and bony, all teeth and elbows. And suddenly awkward, my body becoming unreliable, foreign to me; I was constantly tripping over things, or falling, my legs a mass of bruises, yellow, brown, or freshly purple, graphic testimony to my clumsiness. I saw breasts as the cause of this – the skin slowly, inexorably pinching, rounding, aching, my chest frequently sore. It was the same for Doris. I could see the slight bulges in her blue bathing suit. But we pretended it wasn't happening. Stubbornly I still wore undershirts.

To keep up morale – to ward off the inevitable – we made dumb jokes about "boobs." We called Dubble Bubble gum Dubble Booble. If the water was good for swimming, we said it was "Boobiful." We couldn't stop talking about them.

"I saw Elsie's boobs the other night," I told Doris as we floated peacefully on our inner tubes. I had, and I'd been shocked. I'd burst into her bedroom while she was changing into her nightgown. "They were long and hung down to her waist like a couple of flat inner tubes."

"Eeeew. Ick," Doris said. We both shuddered.

"My grandmother's boobs are as big as two beach balls," she told me. "But I've never seen them naked."

"Lucky you."

We floated some more, gently parting the seaweed and kelp as we went along. Our dogs, Rip and Lucky, were on the beach digging holes. Now and then they'd look up, tracking us, sand all over their noses.

Doris mentioned a girl our age. "Have you seen Brenda Belcher in her new bathing suit?"

"No. Why?"

"It'll make you puke."

"Why? Why?"

"Boobs. Starting at her neck. Going practically all the way to her stomach. Everyone's staring."

"I'd kill myself."

"Me too."

"Or run away from home."

"Yeah."

Instantly, we renamed Brenda Belcher "Big Boobs Belcher."

"Jenny Holt says she was showing her boobs to some boys down on the Point," Doris said.

"What?"

"She said Brenda pulled down the top of her bathing suit and took her boobs out and let the boys stroke them. That's what Jenny said."

I was wildly thrilled with this news. Repelled and fascinated. And I couldn't get over Doris using the word "stroke." What a word! I was jealous.

"What boys?"

"Dunno," Doris said. "Maybe Valerie Kirkendale's cousin and his friends from Victoria. Ask Jenny."

"Was it at night?" I asked. I couldn't imagine the formerly tiny, now voluptuous Brenda Belcher roaming the beach at night; her parents were famously mean and religious.

"Nah. It was Sunday afternoon," Doris said unbelievably.

"Sunday afternoon!"

I pictured Brenda Belcher presenting her breasts like a pair of newborn kittens. With the boys standing hushed and wide-eyed in a semicircle before her. The sun shining, the ordinary day. Small kids farther along the beach playing with shovels and pails. And Brenda saying bossily, "Careful now. Don't squeeze them." The boys on the Point stroking away.

The thought of ever marrying a boy sent Doris and me into fits of gagging.

Doris whispered, "You'd have to ... you know ... *do it* ..."

"No!" I screamed. "Never! Not in a zillion years!"

"Me neither. Wild horses couldn't make me."

We paused, considering.

Then Doris announced, disgusted, "You'd have to wash their dirty underpants."

"Oh! Barf! You'd have to *touch* their dirty underpants!"

"I don't know how my mother stands it," Doris said.

"Oooh. Imagine! You'd have to use tweezers or a stick. To get the underpants into the washing machine. You couldn't touch them with your fingers."

"Think of it," Doris gasped. "Dirty underpants in the laundry basket. Touching your pyjamas. Touching your socks!"

We roamed the neighbourhood looking for washing on clotheslines, evidence to support our repulsion. It was like birdwatching, almost a hobby.

"Look! Over there!" we'd shriek, catching sight of an enormous pair of jockey shorts flapping in the breeze. It was even worse if we could identify the owners: tall Mr. Barlow or fat Mr. Sharp. The very worst thing was to see Mr. Barlow or Mr. Sharp cutting their lawns, or washing their cars, probably wearing the underwear we'd recently spied on their clotheslines. It made us cringe violently to even contemplate such a thing. Once Mr. Sharp waved to us and called, "Hello, girls!" and we ran from him, red-faced, giggling explosively. If we ever had the bad fortune to spot Ernie's underpants on the line, shamefully pinned up there beside my T-shirts and Elsie's slips for the whole world to see, we'd turn away, embarrassed and sickened.

"How can they stand it?" we asked one another, meaning wives. "How can they eat their suppers, do anything?" Because those empty underpants flapping on washing lines like flags at a fair were where a man's *thing* lived. How could a wife eat a meal knowing *that*?

"Why are men's underpants so ... big?" Doris wondered.

"Dunno. Probably because their things are so big. When they grow up, I mean. They turn into elephant trunks."

"Eeeew. Ick!" We laughed.

"I saw Larry Dysart's thing hanging out of his bathing suit last week," I said. "That boy staying next to Mrs. Bland's summer cottage. Why do boys wear those horrible trunks? You can see everything."

Doris had already heard about this. But she asked again, "What did it look like? His thing?"

I'd thought about it a good deal. "Like a little pencil," I said solemnly. I was, after all, delivering a worldly truth. "Like a little, floppy pencil."

"Eeeew. Ick!" Doris said for about the hundredth time that day.

[ELEVEN]

Marion and Jenny Holt

My other best friend, Jenny Holt, lived next door.

At least she had been my friend, I'd lament, back in the good old days
of the previous summer. But within the span of a few winter months
she'd gone from wearing a ponytail and climbing the beach cliffs to
wearing a beehive and driving her mother's car. Somehow it had never
occurred to me that the three-year difference in our ages would lead
to this. Although Elsie had repeatedly warned me, "Jenny's only your
friend because she's late developing."

"Don't say that word!" I'd scream, sticking my fingers into my ears.

"Hah!" Elsie laughed. "There's no stopping it. Once Jenny starts developing, she'll drop you like a hot potato. You just wait till she discovers boys."

That word – "developing." I loathed hearing it. It meant, the dictionary said, "movement from the latent to the active state," a most feeble definition in my opinion. What the word really meant was shocking, gruesome, putrid change, like growing warts or becoming so fat *up there* that you jiggled when you walked and boys stared at you and sniggered. Hearing words like "swollen," "ripe," "mature," "fullness," and even "plum" and "watermelon" made me recoil.

But Elsie was right about Jenny; a pair of revolting breasts had made their appearance on my formerly stick-like friend and done their worst. All the evidence was there; how could I argue with what was plainly going on outside our kitchen window? Boys! And not the twerps I was familiar with, but tall, slouchy, greasy-haired boys. They were a constant sight these days, ushering Jenny in and out of her house as if she were a piece of fragile china. Boys driving their own cars. Boys squealing out of the Holts' driveway, laying rubber along Cordova Bay Road. Now Jenny came to the beach only to demurely sunbathe, towel carefully spread across the sand, baby oil greased meticulously over arms and legs, transistor radio blaring Roy Orbison's whiny hit "Only the Lonely."

Compared to us the Holts were rich. There were the parents, Mr. and Mrs., and the four kids: Sylvia, nineteen; Jenny, sixteen; Valerie, eleven; and Donnie, seven. Their house was much bigger than ours, two full stories, and they had a swimming pool and a horse called Firefly that was kept up the road at the Bar-S Ranch, which was actually a rickety barn with eight horse stalls and not a ranch at all.

Mr. Holt was an accountant with his own firm. Elsie's story about the Holts was this: *They could have lived in the Uplands if they'd wanted to. They have the money. But they don't go in for parties and socializing. They wanted a quiet life.*

Aside from Jenny's defection, I thought the Holts were a perfect family, just like the ones we watched on TV sitcoms – *Father Knows Best, Leave It to Beaver, The Donna Reed Show.* I loved watching those shows. Week after week they laid out a glittery, yet supposedly attainable, parallel universe: beautiful and benevolent mothers, wise dads, pesky but happy children, all contained in neat half-hour stories told with warmth, humour, a soundtrack, and kindly problem-solving at the end. Often Elsie and Ernie would watch these shows with me, the three of us laughing along on cue, enchanted by all that black-and-white happiness. I didn't consider my life that different from those on the sitcoms. I never once formed the thought, "Where are the TV shows about a girl whose mother has 'gone on a long trip,' who has 'flown the coop,' who 'took the last bus out of town,' about a mother who has 'burned her bridges,' is 'frying other fish.' Why are there no laughing audiences for a mother like that?"

But perhaps I was used to living in my own fiction by then. It was a strong fiction, nurtured along by Elsie and the rest of the family – a satisfying kind of Cinderella story, but one without the ashes and the trials, a story that was mostly about ball gowns and liveried coaches, and one where the absent mother was wicked and disdained by all.

Mr. Holt was tall and had crinkly grey hair and soft brown eyes and wore a shirt and tie when he mowed the lawn. But it was Mrs. Holt who enthralled me. She was regal and kind, and I thought of her as a "good queen." She kept house like the TV mothers did, and she wore an apron and high heels and dangly earrings. For her alone I waived my usual disdain for disinfectant-crazed housewives.

Mrs. Holt was the only married woman I'd ever heard call her husband "darling" and "lovey," names that seemed radical to me, flagrantly intimate. One hot afternoon when Mr. Holt was mowing the lawn, I saw Mrs. Holt take him out a glass of lemonade. And then they kissed! A terrible, wonderful sight.

The other amazing thing was that she referred to Jenny and her friends as children, like a storybook mother, like the mother in *Dick and Jane*. "Children," a lovely word, lyrical and pink-cheeked like a song; I felt charmed just hearing it. Outside of Mrs. Holt's sphere everyone called us "kids," a harsh word, a word covered in dirt, a word, in my mind, that meant "nuisance." "You kids, watch what you're doing!" a teacher or a parent or a stranger might holler irritably. "You kids, run out and play!" The word "children" transformed us from irritants into the most endearing creatures. I was astounded by the way an entire scene could suddenly shift like weather, and that one word could be the cause of this.

Mrs. Holt seemed to embody everything that was good, even syrupy sweet, in life. She'd call to us from her back window, "Children, I've made some chocolate-chip cookies." Hearing this would initiate a brief mind-altering experience, a gang of us – her kids and spare kids – charging up the beach trail to her house, then happily munching cookies around her kitchen table. "A cookie and a glass of ice-cold milk! So yummy!" Mrs. Holt would exclaim, practically singing the words. It was like being Anne in an Enid Blyton story set at the English seaside.

"It's just that old recipe off the back of the chocolate-chip package," Elsie sniffed when I reported the rapture I'd experienced in Mrs. Holt's kitchen. "There's nothing special about making those cookies. It's just flour, sugar, and eggs mixed up with the chips." She was icing her renowned brownies and handed me the bowl. "I know for a fact that Mrs. Holt doesn't make these!"

I scraped the bowl with my finger, chocolate icing as light as spun sugar. "It's good," I said.

"Humph," Elsie said. "I should think so."

THERE WAS A FLAW, however, in the otherwise-perfect work of art that was the family next door. They were regular churchgoers and my family wasn't, not by a long stretch. This was the hairline fracture I couldn't avoid taking into account.

"I'd rather hang by my toenails than sit through another sermon," Elsie once remarked, after Billy had said, "God and all that? I could never make sense of the whole shebang."

I'd overheard these things a few months earlier after I was made to go to the Anglican Sunday school up the road – St. David's by the Sea.

"Because you should learn about religion," Billy said seriously when I complained, adding, "It's part of your education."

"Because *we* had to when we were kids," Elsie said, with nasty pleasure, I thought.

During the winter I rode my bike to St. David's Sunday mornings while my family loafed at home. For a while I didn't mind Sunday school. Many of my school friends were there, and it was a refreshing change from *real* school: we could speak out and be rude to the teachers, a pair of helpless, elderly women; chew gum and have bubble-blowing contests; hurl paper planes at each other, gliders made out of pictures of the disciples that we were supposed to be colouring.

But when spring arrived and the beach and the outdoors beckoned, I resented these Sunday mornings and announced that Sunday school was a waste of time. No one seemed interested. All Elsie would say was, "Don't talk to me about it. Billy says you have to go." When Billy was over he said, "Stick it out. You might learn a thing or two."

I started shoving my play clothes out my bedroom window on Sunday mornings, then changing down at the beach and skipping Sunday school. This went on for a couple of weeks. But I soon encountered a problem: with this stolen freedom came boredom and anxiety. Boredom riding around on my bike by myself in the rain in an unfamiliar part of Cordova Bay, where I wouldn't be recognized. Anxiety because I had to keep checking my watch so I could change back into my best clothes and arrive home at the expected time.

As Easter approached I made a fuss, insisting it wasn't fair: "Why am I the only one who has to go to church?"

Reluctantly, Elsie, Ernie, and Billy agreed to attend on Easter Sunday. Bob and Doreen said they'd come along, too; Lyn could go into the infants' class.

During the service, Sunday-school students were allowed to leave the chaos of the "school" room and join the congregation in the church for the last twenty minutes. Everyone's parents were there that Easter Sunday when the group of us trooped in, and for the first time I had the unique experience of feeling I had the same kind of family as everyone else had – a sitcom family!

A pious, dressed up, sitcom family! I was "Kitten" on *Father Knows Best*, the adored youngest child, swinging my legs in the pew, wearing my little white straw hat. I kept glancing around at Elsie, Ernie, Billy, Doreen, and Bob sitting in a row at the back of the church. Elsie and Doreen wore white gloves and hats. The men wore suits. I smiled at them. Tried to catch their eyes. Waved.

I have such a large family, I told myself, thoroughly pleased. They take up an entire pew!

Later, at home, ties were pulled loose, high heels were kicked off, and Easter lunch was served – cold roast beef and potato salad. Seated around the table, the grown-ups started laughing and cracking jokes about Reverend Walsh's sermon.

"Aspic salad!" Elsie cried, wiping her eyes. "When he said that I thought I'd die!"

"I thought I'd wet my pants!" Doreen said.

"I thought I'd wet *my* pants because it was so bloody long," Ernie chimed in. "Having to sit for two hours in church! Like being in prison."

"What I want to know is," Billy added, "what does an aspic salad have to do with the Resurrection?"

No one knew.

"Maybe that's what he thought we'd be having for Easter lunch," Doreen offered.

"Why did he say that?" I asked. "About the Ass-Pick salad."

"Aspic. A-S-P-I-C," Elsie corrected.

"Beats me," Billy said, shaking his head.

"What does Ass-Pick Salad actually look like?" Bob asked cheekily.

"It's made of jelly," Elsie said, smirking. "Red jelly. With bits of carrot and celery in it."

"Oh, Mom, stop it! I can't stand it!" Doreen howled. "Ass-Pick salad."

Everyone roared all over again, and Bob made a show of falling off his chair.

The next Sunday that Billy was over, I flatly refused to go to church. "I'm not going. And you can't make me," I told Elsie and Billy, standing defiantly before them in my play clothes.

They both shrugged; they didn't have a leg to stand on.

I didn't think the Holts' religion was anywhere near as raucous as that of the aspic salad–eating Anglicans. It was called Christian Science, and I knew nothing about it except what Elsie had told me: "They don't believe in drinking or smoking or taking medicine. I can go along with the not drinking or smoking. But not taking medicine? What if someone gets sick?"

I'd once asked Jenny that very question, and she acted embarrassed. "Read the Bible and pray," she said, blushing. "That's what my mother did when Valerie got pneumonia."

I imagined what the Christian Scientists did at their church. It involved a lot of solemn praying and kneeling, not before an altar and cross but before a huge microscope. I thought the minister would wear a lab coat like Mr. Wilson, my science teacher, did, and instead of a sermon, he'd give a demonstration, an experiment with beakers and steam and serious warnings about safety methods.

Often on Sunday mornings after I'd quit Sunday school, Elsie and I would glance out the kitchen window and watch the Holts get into their station wagon for church. At ten in the morning we'd be in slippers and dressing gowns, still puttering about the kitchen getting breakfast. The Holts, of course, would be dressed in their best clothes. Mrs. Holt in particular. She'd be wearing a felt hat and matching green coat with shoulder pads. Herding everyone into the station wagon, she looked like a big green hen. After church I knew they'd be having a family lunch at Paul's Restaurant in Victoria. This was the only part about our neighbours' religion (or any religion) that made me envious – grilled-cheese sandwiches and french fries afterwards in a downtown restaurant.

Elsie would snort, watching them go. "It's a funny religion," she'd say, shaking her head. "And what's the matter with Anglican, I'd like to know? The Holts come from England, after all. That's what *we* were brought up as. If you're from England, that's what you are."

"We're Ass Pickers," I said happily.

"Marion!"

"But, you said ..."

"That was then. This is now."

TWELVE

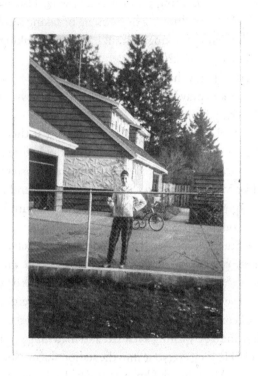

Jenny Holt

Jenny Holt was lying on the beach that day while Doris and I drifted on our inner tubes. She was with the Kirkendale girls, Carol and Sue, older teenagers who, with their younger sister, Valerie, and their parents, summered at a cottage above the Point.

Doris and I sneeringly called Jenny and her friends glamourpusses. They lay on their towels and we couldn't help noticing that their boobs poked out unashamedly from their pink, yellow, and turquoise flowered bathing suits. It was horrible to see. Doris had recently told me that some girls even wore falsies.

"The bigger the better," she'd said.

"What are falsies?" I now asked, again.

"Jeez. I already told you. They're fake boobs. You cut a rubber ball or something in half and stick them on your chest."

I couldn't get over it. "Could you use a dog ball?

"Sure. Or a tennis ball."

"Eeeew. Ick!"

"Yeah. Wonders never cease."

"But wouldn't it hurt?" I persisted. "I mean, how would you stick them on? What kind of glue?"

"How should I know?" Doris said irritably. "It's just what I heard. You buy them in a store."

"In a store? Really? You actually go into a store and say, 'I'll have a set of falsies, please?'"

We laughed.

"Hey, maybe Old Man Smith sells them," Doris said. "Maybe Old Lady Smith wears them." This cracked us up.

Mr. and Mrs. Smith were at least a hundred years old, thin and creaky and sand-coloured, as if they were made of dust. They owned Smith's store halfway down the beach and sold pop, candy, cigarettes, and bread. We were always going in there for Popsicles and bags of penny candy. The Smiths lived in the back of the store and took turns sitting like large, sorrowful birds on a stool behind the counter.

"Hey, after supper let's go ask them," I said. "Let's see what they say."

"Nah. They wouldn't know what we were talking about."

"Dare ya."

"Nah."

"Double dare ya."

"Well ..."

We were out of the water by now and wrapped in towels, hobbling barefoot across the sand and shells. Ahead of us were the older girls. Jenny had turned onto her stomach. Her dark hair was done in a flip with teased wings pointing out several inches on either side of her face. Whenever I saw her these days I looked hard and asked silently, Remember the time we buried treasure in the empty lot beside your house? Remember when we had identical pairs of pink-fluorescent socks and danced to "Blueberry Hill" in your rec room? Remember how only two summers ago you were one of the stars in *Bon Voyage*? You were a matador, and a hula girl, and for the Paris number you wore your mother's high heels and a burlap sack for a sack dress. Remember that? If I really concentrated I could still see her shiny ponytail and the dark thick bangs that hung down over her eyebrows.

In truth I feared this new world that Jenny now so confidently inhabited and avoided even speaking to her. It was as if she'd stepped onto the up escalator in a department store; she had moved fearlessly away from childhood, and me, towards the next level, where all the exciting grown-up experiences were supposed to begin. While I was still in the basement, in the kids' department, hoarding my undershirts, my forts and sandbars, refusing to step onto the escalator myself. Wasn't the grown-up world a grim and confusing place, a battlefield littered with broken promises and broken hearts? Hadn't Nancy and Billy demonstrated this clearly enough? Wasn't it sadness, turmoil, and pretence that lived there?

The new Jenny turned and looked at us as we approached. For some reason I felt embarrassed. By our skinny legs, our dripping hair. By our twerpiness. Carol and Sue ignored us, of course.

"Hi," Jenny said, friendly, as we passed by.

We didn't stop.

"Hi," I mumbled and hurried on.

THIRTEEN

Marion

At home that day after swimming, behind the locked bathroom door, I raised my left arm and made a careful inspection. I had a number of nasty boils there. They were painful to touch, and hot. What had begun as a simple cut had become inflamed, and I was soon hosting an entire family of boils, big ones and little ones, all of them luridly red in colour, like the scary pictures in the medical encyclopedia. My arm hurt every time I moved it. Finally, reluctantly, I showed Elsie.

"What's that?" she gasped. She was in the den knitting a sweater for Lyn, and she jumped up and came towards me. Ernie was watching *Popeye* and paid no attention. Olive Oyl had captured his brain; over and over she was screeching, "Oh, Popeye!"

"Come here to the light. Let me have a look," Elsie said, adjusting her glasses at the window. "Good God! It's infected!"

The panic in her voice made me cry. "It hurts."

"How did you do that?" she demanded, holding my arm and twisting it to get a better look.

"I cut it on a barnacle. Swimming. In between the sandbars. I scraped it out by Seal Rock." She didn't say anything so she must have believed me. I was lying, of course.

"Well I'm calling Dr. Bryant. And you're not going anywhere until that arm is better. Get the Epsom salts down from the cupboard and put on the kettle. You'll have to start bathing it right away." She hurried off to the phone.

I didn't get the Epsom salts. I couldn't face another session at the kitchen table with a bowl of boiling water and a steaming facecloth bathing another infected part of my body – sties, fingers, toes, and now an armpit – with Elsie standing over me bawling, "Are you sure you squeezed out *all* the pus?" I thought she was positively pus crazy. So I didn't move. I sat on the couch and watched Popeye open a can of spinach with his teeth.

"Heh, heh," Ernie said when Popeye's arms miraculously tripled in size. "Heh, heh," he said again when Popeye whacked Brutus so hard he soared all the way to the moon.

I'D CUT MY UNDERARM using Ernie's razor. I didn't know that you needed soap or lather to make a razor blade work smoothly. I'd snuck into the bathroom one Sunday morning when Elsie and Ernie were outside in the garden and locked the door behind me. That was at the end of May, just before Miss Blythe's dance recital. I'd noticed several hairs growing out of each armpit. The sight of them filled me with horror. How could I raise my arms for the final dance? All the classes were included, from the babies to the senior girls. The dance, called "Pas de Swan," was Miss Blythe's version of *Swan Lake*, and I was in a chorus of white swans wearing white-satin tutus. How could I dance before the packed audience at the Royal Theatre with my arms raised in all the important ballet positions? Everyone would see my underarm hair. People on the second floor and even at the back of the balcony would be nudging one other and whispering, "Look at that girl with the hair under her arms! Isn't it repulsive?" Some of the audience would be laughing, "How can she go on stage with all that hair? She looks like a monkey!" And what about Billy, who was coming over from Vancouver midweek especially for the recital? He'd be so ashamed to see me on stage with hairy armpits.

I had to do something.

I found Ernie's black-handled razor in the bathroom drawer. With the first swipe I'd drawn blood; the razor scraped jerkily over my flesh. But I carried on, managing to shave only the left underarm because I kept cutting myself and had to stick on toilet paper to stop the bleeding.

When the time came I performed in the recital with several Band-Aids criss-crossed under my left armpit. The other armpit still sprouted the treacherous hairs. For the finale, the entire dance company was arranged around Sherry Ross, Miss Blythe's favourite pupil that year, who, as the Black Swan, was lying dramatically dead on the stage. The rest of the dancers had their arms above their heads in the final fifth position. Except me. I was the only girl who stood there with her arms clasped by her side.

After the curtain fell and we were rushing off stage, Miss Blythe yanked me by the arm and hissed, "What's the matter with you, standing there like a statue? You ruined the whole number!"

She was about to take her yearly bow in front of the curtain. She'd changed into the red satin gown she wore at the end of each recital and had on her special glasses, the rhinestone-studded ones that were shaped like butterfly wings. Her black hair was backcombed into a stiff French roll and she wore a tiara.

Quaking, all I could think of was, "Now I'll never be Miss Blythe's favourite; now I'll never be picked for a solo part."

In the dressing room I consoled myself with Elsie's usual comment when she thought Miss Blythe was getting too high-strung and uppity around recital time: "In real life she's plain old Mrs. Hammond, and a widow at that. So there's no reason for her to get on her high horse. She's ordinary people like the rest of us. And I don't think she's ever been on a stage herself!"

Every year Miss Blythe called her recital "Stars of Tomorrow." For this year's version, I'd been in three numbers – tap, ballet, and a Russian dance called "Kossak Kaper."

Elsie went all out for Miss Blythe's recital, working for weeks on my costumes. "I've sweated bullets over them," she told everyone, sounding annoyed, but I knew she was proud of her work. "My costumes are always the best," she said frequently. She was an old hand at making costumes for Miss Blythe's recitals, first for Doreen and Shirley, and now for me. She loved it when she could have a free hand with them and design her own colour combinations for the rumba or cancan numbers. "You have to know what colours to pick. What colours stand out on stage," she explained. She favoured lime greens and hot pinks, a certain shade of cherry red she called cerise, and, of course, turquoise.

Driving home that night, with Ernie and Billy in the front seat and Elsie and me in the back, she said loudly, "I thought that Sherry Ross was a bit overdone. Flopping around on stage like a wet seal. Too dramatic. When Doreen was the Black Swan ... I don't know ... she seemed to carry it off better." She raised her voice. "Didn't Doreen do it better, Ernie?"

Ernie, who was driving, said nothing. The dull green light from the dashboard illuminated the top of his head. I could tell he was cranky, though I didn't know why. His hunched shoulders, his tense back. Crankiness wafted from his body in sour waves, filling the car with gloom.

"Cat got your tongue?" Elsie said, half-jokey. Ernie still said nothing, but it was as if Elsie had splashed ice water on him; he flinched, then shuddered.

Billy turned towards the back seat and smiled encouragingly, the anxious peacemaker. "Umm. Yes," he said. "Doreen was good."

I was waiting for him to make a joke, lighten things up the way he often could.

"You weren't even there," Elsie said, now fully peeved. "You were at sea."

She was dressed up for the recital: fur jacket, high heels, and a little black hat with a veil. It had been her night as much as mine. I felt sorry for her. I thought she was going to cry.

"Oh, was I?" Billy said, embarrassed. "Sorry." Leaving the theatre, he'd slipped me a five-dollar bill. "You were good in the Cossak dance," he whispered. The money was still in my hand, limp with sweat.

I piped up, thinking I was on safe, catty ground. "That Sherry Ross is Miss Blythe's favourite. She gets all the best parts. It's not fair."

"You could, too," Elsie snapped. "If you did your part right. Instead of standing there like a block of wood."

Oops.

I tried another tack. "You look just like Ginger Rogers," I said, even though this was plainly untrue; she looked more like a dressed-up teacher or a saleslady. But I knew she admired Ginger Rogers in the late-night movies.

Elsie smiled. "Well I don't know about that," she answered, sounding pleased. Then she hollered at the back of Ernie's greenly glowing head. "Did you hear what Marion said, Ernie? She thinks I look like Ginger Rogers."

Miles went by before Ernie finally spoke. Elsie sat staring out the window at the black night.

"Hah!" he said when he pulled into our driveway. "That's a good one!"

By then no one knew what he was talking about.

I COULD HEAR ELSIE hang up after she finished talking to Dr. Bryant's nurse. It was Monday, breaded-veal-cutlet night; the air was heavy with the familiar smells of fried meat and Raid.

She was soon standing in the den doorway. "You have to go to the doctor's office tomorrow morning," she told me with a mixture of excitement and doom. "He says he'll have to lance those boils. You've probably got a staph infection. You're probably full of pus."

Ernie shot me a glance and gave me the pee-eeew whistle. "Oh, boy," he said next, hammering home his miserable point.

FOURTEEN

Maudie and Grandma

Billy had two older sisters, Elsie and Maudie. From the start it was decided that I should live with Elsie, not Maudie, because Elsie had girls and knew how to raise them. And Maudie didn't. It was as simple as that. She just had "that useless Kenny Pepper." Case closed.

Still, I'd often wonder what my life would be like if the decision had been different. Very comfortable, I decided. Maudie would do everything for me as if I were a princess and she my trusted servant, waiting on me, happily, the way she did for Kenny and Grandma and had done for her husband, Frank, when he was alive. On command she'd scurry to the kitchen, returning with a tray filled with grilled-cheese sandwiches, homemade cookies, hot chocolate, anything I wanted. She'd do my homework, especially the time-wasting social studies projects, roaming the neighbourhood on my behalf to collect different types of leaves for the booklet on trees. When I wasn't lying about reading *Little Lulu* comics, I'd take over the TV set in her living room: only *my* shows would be allowed.

During a recent fight over having to dust my bedroom dresser, I'd screamed, "Maudie would never be so mean. I wish I lived with her!"

"Be my guest," Elsie laughed. "You'd turn out just like Kenny Pepper. We'd call you *that useless Marion Gibson*. A girl who's a slob. A girl who sleeps her life away."

It wasn't hard to compare my aunts: Elsie was strong, and, by default, Maudie was weak. Elsie was also smart, crafty; she knew how things went in the world. You couldn't put anything over on her, and there was safety in that. Whereas Maudie was soft-hearted and kind – or just plain soft – and frequently taken advantage of. Nancy was usually brought up as an example of this. There was the time she stayed at Maudie's house when I was three and never bought groceries and even borrowed money to buy an angora sweater set for herself, money she never paid back. So, though good-hearted, I understood that Maudie was naive and timid, easily manipulated. Elsie, her younger sister, was like a small hurricane. If Maudie was made of pastry dough, Elsie was made of brick. And whose house would you rather be in when the wolf came calling "Little Pig, Little Pig, let me come in"?

Like Maudie and Grandma, Elsie was a small woman, just under five feet tall. "We're short because we didn't get proper nutrition in England when we were kids. You'll be short, too, if you don't eat what's put before you." She'd threaten this so I'd eat the Cream of Wheat or the kidney stew or the lemon-cheese sandwich or whatever else she deemed essential. Cod liver oil in orange juice. Brussels sprouts. Liver.

Short meant being stubby. Never making an impression because you'd be too short to be seen. The dictionary with its satellite meanings – "shortchange," "short-lived," "short-sighted" – was no help either; all of them meant "shortcoming."

Then there was this: to be short *and* without a mind of your own. The possibility that this could be my fate worried me deeply. I'd be practically invisible then – no substance, no thoughts. I feared turning into a short, mindless woman with breasts so huge they'd fit inside a wheelbarrow. I'd have to stay hidden away in the house then, a curiosity, a freak.

Boiled cabbage. Mashed turnips and carrots. I ate it all, to be sure; it was like being an agnostic, covering all bets. Even though I didn't want to grow up, I did want to be a large child. Already I was taller than Elsie, Maudie, and Grandma. As tall as Doreen. But was that tall enough? Doris was taller than me by half a head, and so was Jenny Holt. I'd had a growth spurt, but was that it?

"I was tall at twelve and short at twenty. Sometimes that happens. It's all over before it begins." Another appalling statement from Elsie.

"What about me? I'll be tall, won't I? Nancy's tall."

"Not that tall. She wears high heels. Even to bed."

"But I'm taller than you and I'm only thirteen."

"Your father's short. You could take after him. What makes you think you'll be different?"

"I am different."

"Hah! Just be thankful you're as tall as you are. Keep eating your vegetables."

At thirteen I was five foot two.

"Eyes of blue," Billy sang. "The perfect height for a woman."

"No!"

Perhaps because her size matched neither the largeness nor the force of her character, Elsie made sure she stood out. Her sister and mother wore practical housedresses and aprons and dull Oxford shoes with thick heels. Not Elsie. She had style. Though it wasn't style in the manner of Nancy; there were no fox fur collars on her coats and she didn't use a cigarette holder or wear shoes with dice floating in the heels. Elsie's style, rather, was in the way that she managed, because of her sewing skill, to be something she called "well presented."

She made most of our clothes – Doreen's, Shirley's, hers, mine – from the Butterick and Simplicity catalogues, favouring patterns that "lengthened" you, made you seem as tall as the drawings of the elongated models in the book: A-line dresses, coats with long, flowing lines, pedal-pushers worn with high heels. I'd often find her in her bedroom hunched over the sewing machine, absorbed in her work, a cigarette hanging from the side of her mouth, the ash a precarious two inches in length and threatening to fall on the length of seam flying along beneath her fingers. Now that Ernie no longer shared the bedroom, it had become a sewing centre. A bench ran along one side of the double bed, Ernie's former side; the wooden ironing board with the thick flannelette cover stood nearby and was never taken down. She worked away in her room, furiously, sometimes for hours at a time, often well into the night. Now and then Ernie or I would call to her. "Come see what's on TV!" But she'd refuse: "I'm too busy!" Or not answer at all. The stop-and-go wail of the sewing machine was so loud at times, so annoying, that it drowned out *Gunsmoke* or *Zorro* and Ernie or I would have to turn up the TV.

Maudie sewed only dolls' clothes – for my dolls when I was younger, and now for the baby Lyn's future dolls. There was a shoebox in her linen closet that awaited Lyn's possession; it was filled with folded doll dresses, coats, underpants, and pyjamas, and also knit sweaters and bonnets in delicate lacy patterns. It was like a doll's trousseau, a marvel. Maudie would often, at my request, bring the clothes out to show me, laughing at the silliness of a frill sewn around a skirt, the absurdity of tiny puff sleeves.

The other thing Maudie did was act as keeper of the family albums. When she showed us pictures from them she'd tell stories about their childhoods in Liverpool, England. Like Elsie's stories, Maudie's almost had titles: "Yes, We Were Poor, But ..." (the fun the kids had sharing bathwater). "The Strange Things We Ate" (tripe, brains, fried bread). "What We Got for Christmas" (one present each: socks or a ball). "Our Birthday Cakes" (pound cake, no icing). She laughed all the way through each story as though their early poverty were the most delightful thing in the world. Pictures would erupt in my mind like illustrations in old-fashioned books, quaint, amusingly simple, jolly. The funny clothes people wore, their strange, square cars, the streets filled with crowds walking about jerkily like people did in silent movies. "The Way My Mother Washed Clothes" (tub and boiling water). "The Times My Father Disappeared." Even my grandfather was given a playful touch: "After three days Ma and me would go looking for him. And usually find him asleep on a bench at the train station ..." The only other things I knew about my grandfather were that he'd been an orphan in Ireland, and that he was too drunk to walk Elsie down the aisle when she married Ernie; Billy had to.

Grandma usually sat at the end of the vinyl-covered table in Maudie's kitchen playing solitaire, no longer the person of the stories. No longer even remembering the stories, it seemed, because she never contributed to them, never commented. Poverty forgotten. Immigration to Canada in 1920 forgotten. A binge-drinking husband forgotten. But she still poured full bottles of beer and glasses of rye and ginger down the sink any chance she got.

Maudie's house was in Saanich, four miles from Cordova Bay, and it was as if our car were on a permanent track between her house and ours. You could almost let the car drive itself, pretend it was a horse that knew the way. We seldom went anywhere else – Cordova Bay to Lake Hill and back again. Four Ways Market was up the road from Maudie, and Len, the butcher there, with his father before him, had been the family butcher for forty years. When I was thirteen Maudie's husband, Frank, had been dead for eleven years. He was a mean man, I was told, so it was a blessing when he died. This was Elsie's story, not Maudie's. "When Frank Died."

The day after his body was removed from Maudie's double bed – he'd had heart disease – she and Grandma got to work with a pail of hot water and a bottle of bleach. They scrubbed everything – the mattress, the bed frame, even the walls. Then Maudie went out and bought new sheets and a new bedspread. And Grandma moved into the bed, into the spot Frank had just vacated. Now instead of Frank's cigarettes and ashtray on the bedside table, it was Sloan's Liniment and Grandma's teeth in a jar.

Once a month Maudie and Grandma visited Ross Bay Cemetery in

Victoria to polish the graves – my grandfather's and Frank's. I'd often go along because Billy, Elsie, or Ernie was driving; Kenny was seldom awake in time. No matter what the month, a cold wind blew off the Strait of Juan de Fuca that bordered the cemetery, and we'd stand beside the graves shivering while Maudie got down on her hands and knees and scrubbed the plaques – *In loving memory of* ... (It was considered rude to stay warm inside the car.) Then she'd dump out the old flowers from the rusted tin and Grandma would hand her fresh ones: roses from the garden if it was summer, holly or branches of snowberry if it was winter. Sometimes Maudie would pack a thermos of tea and a tin of cookies and we'd sit on the cement curb beside the car having a small picnic there in the graveyard; no one else was ever about. Around us there were tall moss-covered tombstones tilting with age, and mown grass between the graves, neat as a park; there were overhanging arbutus trees with smooth red trunks that shed brittle leaves in the wind. The sea glimpsed through the trees was choppy, cold grey, goosebump grey, water so cold it would numb your ankles in a second.

Maudie laughed before, during, and after these visits to the cemetery, and it was a delighted laugh, as if she were doing something wonderful – going on a rare vacation, or attending an afternoon tea.

I came to understand that this is what happened after you died. There were no tears. Just the brisk tidying of your grave. A little polish, some flowers. Cookies and a thermos of tea beneath swaying firs and cedars. Sometimes laughter. Sometimes giddy delight over a day that always seemed so surprisingly bright.

[FIFTEEN]

Grandma, Nancy, Marion

We were sitting in Maudie's kitchen. I'd just had my boils lanced in Dr. Bryant's Victoria office and was still smarting from that ordeal. The nurse, with Elsie's help, had had to hold me down while Dr. Bryant, who was so old his bushy white eyebrows were stained yellow, worked on me with a razor-sharp blade. I'd screamed and fought. Mopping up afterwards, the doctor had asked the nurse and Elsie, "Ever seen so much pus?" He sounded excited. "Never!" they'd both exclaimed, wide-eyed.

Maudie's kitchen was a place snugly familiar to me, with its pale-yellow walls and worn linoleum floor. She and Grandma, Elsie and I were squeezed around the tiny wooden kitchen table that was shoved between the window and the fridge. Looking outside it was hard to believe it was June 28, nearly the last day of school. The weather had suddenly changed; it was more like November. The sky was low and dark, and heavy rain hammered the fruit trees in Maudie's back garden. Inside her kitchen, the oil stove was roaring and the windows were steamed.

Grandma was perched in her usual place, the corner seat at the table, and she had the cards laid out for solitaire. The teapot and tin of cookies were in the centre of the table and Maudie was acting excited; pink dots appeared on both of her cheeks like clown spots. She was excited, I knew, because of having visitors, even though our visit was nothing new. But she was acting the way she always did when someone dropped by, as if your visit were the best thing in the world, the thing that made her day. She was an energetic woman with deep-set brown eyes and a prominent hook nose, and she always seemed to be running everywhere – inside her house, in her garden, even shopping for groceries up the road. "Slow down," Elsie often cried out. "You'll break your bloody neck."

My cousin Kenny was there that day, too, though asleep in the basement. He was often asleep – at eleven in the morning, at two in the afternoon – the time didn't matter.

"He's a night owl," Maudie would explain. Elsie always rolled her eyes when she heard this.

Kenny was twenty-nine years old and still lived at home with his mother and grandmother, although nothing was really the matter with him, he was just a boy who never moved out on his own or a man who overstayed his welcome, depending on who was telling the story. This fact, I knew, contributed to his being called useless. Not having a regular job didn't win him any points either.

I was reading the *Betty and Veronica* comic Elsie had bought me after the visit to Dr. Bryant's office and was peacefully working my way through a stack of cookies when Elsie suddenly said, "You're just like your father. Always got your nose in a book."

I was about to defend myself, tell her that a comic was not a book, but then I caught her sighing – half-smiling – and knew she was beginning a story.

Right out of nowhere she said, "I knew it wouldn't work."

"What?"

"Your mother and father. Nancy and Billy. I knew right from the start. He was very bookish, always had his nose stuck in a book. Like you," she said. "He wanted to be quiet and read every night and your mother wanted to kick up her heels and have a good time."

The women in Billy's family, his mother, sisters, and nieces, were fiercely loyal to him, and protective. Only occasionally would they concede that he might have been less than a perfect husband. And being "bookish" was a substantial fault.

"He was tired from working on the docks all day," Maudie protested gently. "All those long hours supervising the boats. Of course he'd want a nice supper, and then to put his feet up."

"Nice supper! Hah!" Elsie said crossly. "Nancy couldn't boil an egg. If there was any supper, Billy made it."

Maudie shook her head and looked sad. She hated hearing bad things about people, even if they were true.

Grandma said nothing. She was absorbed with the cards and chewing on her lower lip. Snap: red queen on black king.

"And Nancy borrowed money from everyone. From all of us," Elsie continued, lighting another cigarette. "Remember that angora sweater set? How much did she borrow from you for that? Twenty dollars?" Maudie made a clicking sound at the back of her throat; Elsie paused, seemingly in thought. Cigarette smoke drifted in thin bands across the teapot. "And she hated Grandma," she resumed. "They fought like cats and dogs. Isn't that right, Ma?"

Hearing her name, Grandma looked up. But her face was blank.

Maudie smiled sheepishly.

"Why did they fight?" I cried. "What did they say?" This was exciting news. Like cats and dogs? I couldn't imagine Grandma fighting with anyone; she was so crinkly and old.

"I don't remember what they said," Elsie answered. "But it was about money, that's for sure. It was when you and Nancy were staying with Grandma for a few weeks. That time Billy was out on the boats. You were only a year old. Nancy borrowed a hundred dollars from Grandma to buy you a buggy. Told her she needed to take you out for walks. But she bought herself a string of pearls and matching earrings instead. She was jealous of Billy's old girlfriend, Ruth Parkinson, who was married to Billy's friend Tom. They got together as couples a few times. Nancy wanted to show herself off before Ruth, who was a good-looking girl, tall with long, dark hair. She got the pearls at the Hudson's Bay Company. Paid cash with Grandma's money. I was with her when she bought them. I said, 'Nancy, what about Marion's buggy?' But she acted like she hadn't heard me. She was all dolled up, with that fox fur around her neck, and telling the saleswoman she was the wife of a captain. 'My husband is Captain W.D. Gibson,' she said. The saleswoman couldn't have cared less." Here Elsie let out an incredulous laugh. "Grandma had it out with her over that necklace. A real shouting match. But after that she wouldn't speak to her. If Nancy came into the room, Grandma would get up and leave. Nancy started calling her an old biddy behind her back. It took Billy years to pay off Nancy's debts. Remember those pearls, Maudie?"

I looked hard at Maudie. She shrugged her shoulders and had that "What can you do?" look on her face. I wanted her to say something, because when she told stories she laughed all the time and everything was so happy. Elsie's stories always had a bitter edge to them. I stared at Maudie eagerly until she spoke. "Well," she said finally, "Nancy sure knew how to wear clothes."

"I'll give her that," Elsie conceded. "But she'd never show her face until she'd put on her makeup. You wouldn't believe the things she put on her face. Had a special suitcase just for her makeup. I'd never seen such things."

"She was pretty," Maudie said simply.

"Because of all the makeup," Elsie repeated, irritated. It was plain to her that Nancy would be nothing without her makeup. Why wasn't it plain to Maudie? "Without makeup, Nancy looked like a limp dish rag. And her hair! It was so thin. She couldn't do a thing with her hair. But I knew it wouldn't work," Elsie swept on. "Nancy and Billy. Two more different people you couldn't imagine. It was doomed right from the start. Billy should have married Ruth Parkinson when he had the chance."

This was the first time Elsie had used the word "doomed" in telling the story, although I'd heard about the pearls and Ruth Parkinson before. Briefly, I considered myself as a "doomed daughter," but I couldn't create a suitably bleak image because I was feeling too glad now that summer was about to begin, even if it was raining out, even if I was banned from swimming for two weeks because of the boils. And it didn't bother me that Billy hadn't married Ruth Parkinson. The chance that I might not have existed didn't occur to me.

But it did to Maudie. "Good thing he didn't marry Ruth," she said, looking at me and smiling.

"Well, that goes without saying," Elsie snorted.

Then the subject changed to knitting patterns and the story was over. I decided to climb down Maudie's steep basement stairs and wake up Kenny.

SIXTEEN

Maudie and Grandma

Kenny's room was deep in Maudie's basement, half
underground. A window near the ceiling let in weak, dusty light. It
was dingy in there, with the moose head on the wall and the framed
pictures of pagodas Kenny had brought back from the Korean War.
Calendars with half-naked girls selling engine oil or the services of
barbers or mechanics were tacked up around the room. Kenny never

tore off the month-by-month pages from these calendars; there were different years, but every calendar said "January."

Kenny was asleep on a single bed and covered with heavy cream-coloured blankets. I thought he slept so much because he stayed up late practising to become Victoria's Elvis Presley. There was a contest that summer and Kenny said he was thinking about entering it. You had to look like Elvis and do all the moves like Elvis and pretend to sing one of his hit songs. And if you won, you were crowned "The King" and given a one-hundred-dollar bill. Then you got to ride on a float in the May Day Parade the following spring.

"Have you entered the contest yet?" I'd ask anxiously. "Did you get your name in before the deadline?"

"Maybe, maybe not," Kenny would say evasively.

"Why haven't you?" I'd plead, picturing the glory I'd have: my cousin, Victoria's Elvis Presley!

"Don't waste your breath," Elsie told me. "He's not going to enter. He wouldn't stand a chance. He's too short. You have to be tall."

"But he'd win!"

"He wouldn't get up in time," Elsie continued, as if this reason alone supplanted all others. "He'd wake up in the middle of the afternoon and it would all be over. You can't win a contest if you sleep through the bloody thing."

I stood beside the sleeping Kenny amid the refuse of the previous night – empty Coke bottles, a plate with the remains of a ham sandwich that Maudie had made for him before she went to bed, dirty socks and jeans lying on the floor, his guitar and records. His blond hair stuck out from beneath the covers. He wore his hair like Elvis Presley, of course, carefully greased and piled on his head, with a single seductive curl falling over his forehead. With sleeping, though, his stiff hair would lose its shape, crack apart, so that the long blond thickness with the curl attached now appeared to be lying beside his head on the pillow like a small animal, a pet mouse perhaps.

I poked him. I thought if I could wake him up, even if it was late morning, he'd become used to the idea and make it a habit; then he'd be up in time to enter and win the contest.

"C'mon, Kenny, get up. It's almost afternoon."

I wanted to see him practise being Elvis Presley, too. He was good at it. The way he swivelled his hips, shocking Grandma. The way he stuck out his lower lip and nodded his head in time to "Blue Suede Shoes" always made me laugh. He wore his jeans so low down you could see the crack in his behind whenever his white T-shirt pulled away during practice sessions. And always there'd be a turquoise plastic tail comb sticking out of his back pocket. That summer, when Kenny was being Elvis Presley, he went around calling grown-up women "ma'am," just like the real Elvis did in the movies. "Yes, ma'am," he'd say, even to his own mother when she asked him if he wanted more mashed potatoes. "Yes, ma'am. Don't mind if I do."

Kenny was a small man and, like Billy, slightly built. When I was thirteen, we were the same height. Although Elsie was right – he was short – I didn't see this as a problem. Because he was so cocky and self-assured around the house, and so much fun to be with, laughing over everything the way Maudie did. Surely this would translate onto a stage as well.

Now in his room there was the smell of dirty socks and Aqua Velva aftershave lotion mixed with dust from the moose head and damp from the cement walls. But something else was there, too, another smell, musty and alarmingly male. When he didn't move I poked him again, on his arm and his foot, careful to avoid the hair on the pillow and particularly the middle part of his body where another mouse – or was it an elephant trunk? – lay curled and sleeping; you had only to touch it and it would pounce on you and somehow destroy your life.

Finally, Kenny turned and looked at me with bewildered, squinty eyes. He groaned, raising himself awkwardly on one elbow, and cautiously licked his cracked lips before he spoke. His tongue was covered with white fur and his eyes would not focus. Then he croaked in my direction, "Get lost, Squirt," and collapsed into his nest of pillows.

"You have to get up and practise," I pleaded, shaking his bed with my foot. "For the contest. You can't win if you stay in bed all day."

"Go away," he mumbled.

Climbing back upstairs was like returning from a failed mission, and I whined to Maudie, "Why is Kenny sleeping all the time? He's no fun anymore. He'll never be Victoria's Elvis Presley."

Elsie grunted, took a long drag off her cigarette, and looked at me with her "my lips are sealed" look, which I knew meant, "Kenny sleeps all day because he's a lazy good-for-nothing who doesn't have to lift a finger because his mother does everything for him and would even wipe his bum if he told her to."

"Eh?" Grandma said.

"Kenny," I yelled. "He's always sleeping."

She looked at me, stunned. She was holding the ten of diamonds in her hand, and then she snorted. I wondered if she'd heard me. Recently I'd watched a TV show about how to read lips and that this was something deaf people could do to keep their deafness a secret. But Grandma became annoyed whenever I insisted she look at me while I spoke; she refused to read my lips. "Oh, go away with you," she'd say, waving her hand.

But then a surprise! She'd heard my question about Kenny. "Let him sleep," she said, sounding completely ordinary. "It's the only time I don't have to listen to that music he plays. That racket. I have to go sit in the bathroom to get any peace and quiet."

"What do you do in the bathroom?" I hollered, exaggerating each word slowly, still hoping she might read my lips. I struggled into the chair beside her.

"Don't shout," Elsie said, looking up from her knitting book.

"I'm not."

I was picturing Grandma sitting on the toilet with a tray on her lap, the cards for solitaire laid out; Grandma, small and wide in her black house dress and thick beige stockings, sitting very still, careful not to tip the tray. For hours and hours. Maudie's toilet was decorated with a fuzzy pink toilet-lid cover. A doll with a crocheted pink-and-white skirt sat on the tank lid hiding a spare roll of toilet paper beneath her skirt.

"Eh, Grandma? What do you do in the bathroom?"

She looked at me, exasperation on her face, and said, "Sheesh." Then returned to the cards, humming a line from her favourite nursery rhyme, "Four and twenty blackbirds baked in a pie ..."

Maudie looked at the clock. "Cripes," she laughed, jumping up. "It's nearly twelve thirty!" This was an amazing occurrence for her, and for all of us. To actually be late fixing lunch! To have time slip by unnoticed, a full half-hour unaccounted for, noontime abandoned, forgotten. She raced to the cupboard and grabbed two tins of cream of chicken soup and a tin of canned salmon. That's what she and Grandma and Kenny, if he was up in time, had for lunch every day: chicken soup and salmon sandwiches. For breakfast, it was Cream of Wheat and toast, and for supper, a piece of fried meat with mashed potatoes and boiled carrots and home-canned green beans. Bird's Custard flowing like yellow lava over canned fruit or sliced bananas was what they had for dessert.

Maudie was giddy, the red dots on her cheeks exploding to cover the bridge of her nose and her chin. Elsie caught the mood, and, laughing, leaped up to help make the sandwiches, hastily covering slices of white bread with a thick layer of butter. You'd think someone was going to march in and shout at them for not making lunch on time.

Later, as we were in the car pulling out of Maudie's driveway, Elsie started talking. "That Kenny Pepper!" she said harshly. "A grown man still living with his mother. Oh, it galls me the way Maudie waits on him hand and foot."

I both liked and hated hearing Elsie talk about Kenny Pepper. Liked the feeling of being Elsie's confidante. Hated feeling like a betrayer. Of Maudie's kindness and good humour, of her steamy and cozy kitchen. And of Kenny and the excitement about the Elvis Presley contest. I was certain he could win; all he had to do was get up in time.

"I think it's nice," I said cautiously, peering sideways, watching Elsie's tight, angry face. Her cigarette hung out the side of her mouth, and when she pulled it away from her lips, banging the ash against the car ashtray, there was a bright smear of red lipstick on the filter. I could never figure out why Kenny made her so mad; she wasn't the one who had to look after him.

"I think it's *really* nice," I continued, bolder now. "Look how happy he makes Maudie." I had observed this much: the "useless Kenny Pepper" was the apple of his mother's eye. So my defence was simple and

I felt virtuous, resting my case. Who could compete with happiness and love?

"You don't know what you're talking about," Elsie snapped. "You don't know a damned thing." And she launched into her "When Frank Was Alive" story.

When Frank was alive it was the same. Maudie was his slave. She was always nervous, fidgety, trying to please him. It's what she lived for. I used to try and get her to go out with me, shopping or to the park. But everything depended on what Frank was doing. "Oh, no," she'd say. "Frank will be wanting his lunch." Or, "Frank will be wanting to work in the garden." Meaning she'd be doing most of the work. The weeding, the hauling wheelbarrows of dirt. While he'd maybe prune the apple tree, then sit on a lawn chair with a bottle of beer and watch her. And she's the same with Kenny. Waiting on him. Now she's got to stay around the house all morning because Kenny will want feeding when he decides to drag himself out of bed. Or she's got to buy only butter because Kenny won't eat margarine. It's the same bloody thing. The same bloody record.

She was quiet then, puffing away, driving my father's car, the small grey-and-blue Zephyr he'd bought for her to use because, she said, we lived in the sticks and how could she grocery shop and take me to dancing lessons from a place where there was no bus? Ernie's dirty old pickup wouldn't do; she refused to drive it. "Can you picture me climbing into *that*?" she hooted. She wore high heels and stockings practically every day, and it was true, no one could imagine her driving a truck.

SEVENTEEN

Marion and Maudie

cA dirt trail midway along the stretch of Cordova Bay beach led to Smith's store. This trail also doubled as the public beach access. There was a small parking lot beside the store and a park with swings that fronted the road. Where the path met the beach was a rough wooden building, painted green, that housed change stalls and a row of stinky toilets.

The beach here was littered in summer with pale families spread out on wool blankets having their lunches – bottles of Coke or Orange Crush and floppy white-bread sandwiches. People out for the day, chancing the tides and the weather, city people. Doris and I pitied the kids who were always hysterical at the beach, trying to cram everything into one measly afternoon as if it were their last day on earth. Everything they did was frantic: digging in the sand with their plastic shovels; balancing on driftwood logs; throwing wet sand at each other; gobbling ice cream cones or Popsicles from Smith's store; building sandcastles and anxiously waiting for the incoming tide so they could watch them disintegrate. And then, just when they'd relaxed enough to have some real aimless fun, they'd be shouted at and told to pack up, head for the car, and don't be slow about it. These were kids whose bodies were shamefully white or blotchy red with sunburn. Their fathers, wearing white undershirts and rolled-up pants that exposed their gnarly feet, slept after lunch with newspapers spread over their faces. Their mothers wore cotton housedresses – never shorts or bathing suits – and spent the entire beach time hollering at their kids to stay close to shore. We pitied them all. It didn't occur to us that none of the grown-ups in our lives ever spent a full day at the beach. But they lived there, so they didn't have to; we didn't expect it. And it would have been intrusive to have them swimming and sunbathing near us. It would have seemed strange.

THE WEATHER HAD CHANGED again, the rain of the previous days giving way to clear skies. It was hot now, just in time for Dominion Day on July 1, when Elsie had planned a family supper. School was over for the year, and though I couldn't swim because of the thick underarm bandage I still wore, I could wade or float on my inner tube.

Doris and I were sitting on the Point after a long float in the water.

"We're the lucky ones," she was saying, looking calmly at the crowd of bathers huddled around Smith's beach access. We could see their dismal shapes. Watching them, Doris added, "Think how cruddy it would be in the city."

This was a favourite theme: how lucky we were to live at Cordova

Bay all year round. Even summer kids like the Kirkendale girls had to return to Victoria at the end of August. We felt sorry for them, too. Because we had it so much better. We had this wild and beautiful place, tree filled and remote, practically to ourselves. So what if we lived in the sticks? So what if there were no buses or sidewalks or street lights? Same for movie houses or proper stores. We had the glorious beach, summer and winter. And the dirt road above the main road called the Track, which had once been a railway line, and the woods beyond sloping up the hill away from the sea. We had the entire length of Cordova Bay Road. This was ours to race along on our bikes with our hair flying, our dogs panting beside us, anytime we wanted.

"Yeah," I said. "City kids have the worst luck. They have to go to public pools or boring parks. Or maybe they get to go to the beach one day a year. Whoopee ding."

"Or Bible camp," Doris said.

We both shrieked, "Bible camp!"

We'd heard about Bible camp from Brenda "Big Boobs" Belcher, who went there for two weeks every summer.

"We have to sleep on metal cots," she'd told us primly, "and we only get one blanket and we have to pray all the time and the only fun is afternoon crafts, sticking macaroni letters onto pieces of wood. Mine said, 'Suffer the Little Children.'"

"Suffer," I said. "You got that right."

"Why don't you run away?" Doris asked practically.

Brenda looked stunned. "Run away? But I like it!"

"Like it?"

"Yes. I like it."

Afterwards I'd phone Doris up. "Wanna play Bible camp?"

"Oooh, yes," she'd scream.

But playing Bible camp never lasted long now. It was mainly making fun of Brenda Belcher's new boobs, because we couldn't think of anything else to do.

Shielding our eyes from the sun, we watched a group of smaller kids building sandcastles. I started counting turquoise bathing suits. "Two. Three."

"How come only girls have turquoise bathing suits?" I asked.

"Search me," Doris said, sounding bored. Her bathing suit was blue but counted as "almost turquoise" because her mother had said, cruelly we thought, that her old suit still fit and she wasn't wasting good money on a new one. My bathing suit was gloriously turquoise with thick, vertical white stripes.

Doris sighed, and I wondered what was the matter with her. Then she perked up. "There's the Bethells!"

"So?"

Down by Smith's store, Robert and Raymond, brothers, thirteen and fourteen, were dragging their boat across the sandbar to the water. Like us, they were year-round residents and they went to our school. And like us, anyone could tell they were true beach kids. They were lithe and muscular and evenly tanned; their hair was sun-bleached, golden and silver-white.

Doris grabbed her towel and thongs. "Let's go see what they're doing."

"What for?"

"Maybe they'll give us a ride in their boat. Or take us water-skiing."

I looked at her, instantly suspicious. Who was this person? Where was my boob-hating, boy-hating pal? Her red hair was wet and curly and her face was glowing – tanned and burned and freckled all at once. She looked almost pretty.

"Nah," I said, scratching around the tape on my bandage. I made a show of watching some gulls land on Seal Rock.

"C'mon. Don't be such a sourpuss."

"Why? Do you like Raymond Bethell or something?"

"No way!" she shrieked. I felt relief. "But Robert Bethell's kind of cute."

"Doris!"

"Well, he is. And Raymond likes *you*."

Beyond my control, a feeling of pleasure erupted from my stomach and left me feeling bewildered. Where had that come from? It made me want to grin but at the same time left me feeling wildly upset. "That's a lie! You're making it up!" Then added, because I couldn't help myself,

"How do you know?"

Doris was delighted with my interest. She started giggling and acting goofy. What was so funny? "Robert told me," she laughed, overwhelmed with pleasure.

"You were talking to Robert Bethell all by yourself?"

"So?" she snapped. "Don't be such a baby." She was angry and impatient with me now. "I'm going down the beach," she announced. "You can stay stuck here if you want to." And left me gaping after her.

I wanted to shout at her, call her stuck-up, anything but what she suddenly, unbelievably appeared to be – a betrayer, a boy-crazy betrayer. But in my shock I merely followed along, several strides behind. She'd wrapped her towel around her waist like a skirt and strode heavily towards the boys on the beach.

I soon caught up and we walked in silence. I didn't want to meet up with the brothers, and luckily we were too late to catch them. They'd already launched their boat; it was bobbing farther out on the water. Robert or Raymond Bethell – I couldn't tell which – was bent over the engine, pulling the cord, trying to get it going.

Doris picked up a shell and threw it at me. She'd softened. "Raymond Bethell thinks you're cute," she said. "Robert told me."

"Don't make me puke." I shoved her arm, not sure why I was grinning now.

"I bet you like him, too. Don't you?"

"I do not. He's a boy, isn't he?"

"You do! I can tell. You're blushing! Who would have thought it? Wonders never cease."

"It's not true," I yelled and started running back down the beach.

"Hey, Marion! Wait up! Don't have a bird. I was only kidding."

I kept on running.

WHEN I GOT HOME I headed for the bathroom and locked the door behind me. I was curious to look in the mirror. I wanted to see what Raymond Bethell had seen. I wanted to see what "cute" looked like. I stared at my face. Was it cute? I smiled at my reflection, looking closely at the way my face was evenly tanned, the way the hair around my forehead was bleached white. I turned sideways and studied my profile, laughing silently at my reflection, allowing myself to be charmed by the words: *Raymond Bethell thinks you're cute!* I swung my ponytail, stiff with seawater. I pouted, struck poses like the ones on Kenny's calendars, tried different ways of smiling. With or without teeth? In turn I scrutinized my eyes (green), ears (ordinary), hair (long and scraggly), and nose (just a nose). But didn't cute girls have turned-up noses? It certainly wasn't my "figure," which, thankfully, was still like a boy's, straight as a board and, if I rounded my shoulders, with not a boob to defile it. Maybe it was my personality. Having a "perky personality" was something old Miss Gillenspence, the grade seven guidance teacher, said was prized by the opposite sex. But I'd always rejected this notion; as far as I was concerned, a "perky personality" meant being an idiot – a chattery girl, someone who was dumb beyond hope. It was baffling.

Elsie hollered at me from the hallway. "What are you doing in there?"

"Nothing."

"Well, come out. I've got something to tell you."

I opened the door a crack. "What?"

"Your father phoned. He'll be on the seven ferry. Up the road at quarter to nine."

"I know that," I snarled. "He's coming a day early because of the holiday, isn't he?"

"Well, you don't know everything. You're not that smart. There's something else." She paused. "He got a phone call from your mother. She's coming for a visit."

"What?"

"She's on a cruise ship that's docking in Los Angeles. She's going to fly up to the Island. She'll be here in two weeks."

"What?"

"Don't keep saying that. You heard me the first time. As if I didn't have enough on my plate. And now our trip to Grand Coulee Dam is going to be ruined on top of everything else. Ernie only has two weeks off. And Maudie was really looking forward to the trip. I don't know what we're going to do. Trust Nancy to spoil everything."

EIGHTEEN

Elsie, Nancy, Grandma, Marion, Maudie

Elsie and Ernie watched me during supper. Every time I looked up from my fried fish and boiled potatoes, they were staring.

"What? What?"

"Nothing."

We ate in silence. The fridge chugged and wheezed. Rip, chained to his doghouse, barked. Ernie made sloppy chewing sounds and then picked his teeth with a fingernail. A car backed noisily out of the Holts' driveway. Elsie smacked the end of the ketchup bottle, trying to hurry up the pour.

I knew I was supposed to be having a reaction to the news of Nancy's visit. Knew that I was supposed to be displaying some sort of emotion. This is what Elsie and Ernie were expecting. But which emotion should I be having? Dismay? Excitement? Happiness? Anger? What? The truth was I felt nothing then. Only that I was hungry. That I wanted to eat my supper. That I was anxious to make up with Doris. That I didn't want to think about any of this.

Finally, Elsie broke the spell when she served the ice cream and canned peaches for dessert. "You'd think we could have had more warning," she said in her "spitting mad" voice. "Just like that, Her Ladyship decides to pay a visit!"

"Oh well," Ernie said.

"Oh well, nothing! We don't see Nancy for eight years and she decides to drop in like she's been out shopping? The nerve of some people. The bloody gall. And where are we going to put her? That's what I want to know. Where's she going to sleep? You know Grandma hates her. She can't stay at Maudie's. And on top of everything she's ruined our holidays. Did you think about that? Did that even cross your mind?"

Ernie shrugged.

"Well?"

"Maybe I can change them. My holidays. For two weeks in September ..."

"September! What good is September? Marion will be in school then. And Billy can't get off. That's his busy time. September's the most ridiculous thing I've ever heard of."

"Nag, nag," Ernie said, which is what he always said when cornered. He threw down his napkin and left the table, his half-uneaten dessert a soup of melted ice cream and peach syrup.

It was comforting to hear them bicker like this – so normal, so every-day. And it was a relief to hear Elsie's comments about Nancy's visit. She'd struck exactly the right mood, and it was a mood I immediately adopted. Elsie had handed me a road map for my emotions, a plan for how I'd act about the confusing and shocking news: put out, annoyed, inconvenienced. Following Elsie's lead, then, this is how I would be. I would take the familiar position: family life as a Wild West show with circled wagons – *Wagon Train* – and the bad guys (Nancy) kept at bay, kept "out there."

So Elsie, in her oblique way, had settled things at once. I wore her opinion like a dress she'd made especially for me. Now I didn't have to think any further about Nancy's arrival; nothing, it seemed, was expected of me. There was just one thing, though: Billy. Billy gave me an ache of worry. Billy and his broken heart.

After supper I phoned Doris.

"Whatcha doing?"

"Nothing."

"Wanna come over? Go down the beach?"

"Dunno."

"Sorry about this afternoon."

"S'okay."

We headed for the Point. The tide was so high that the rocks lower down had vanished. The sea looked swollen, overbrimming, as if the bay were a huge bowl that couldn't be filled with any more water.

"Those stupid old Bethells," Doris began when we'd settled on the rocks. "Who cares about them anyway?"

"Yeah."

"They're just cruddy boys."

"Yeah."

We sat for a while saying nothing and watched a sailboat farther out. Our dogs, sensing the gloomy quietness, sat beside us. I patted Rip. "Good old boy."

"Whaddya wanna do?" Doris asked.

"I dunno. Whatever you want to do."

"I don't care. I'll do what you want."

We did nothing. We could hear the Kirkendales laughing on their deck above us. Two families shared the summer cottage and were often playing card games together, kids and adults. The sound of that laughter made me want to cry.

"My mother's coming to visit," I said. "On an ocean liner. Then on a plane from Los Angeles."

"Holy," Doris said. "I thought you were still mad at me."

"Nah."

"When's she coming?"

"In two weeks. All the way from Australia. She'll probably be bringing her jewels and fur coats. She's probably got a new husband, too. She's really rich, you know."

"Yeah, I know. Lucky you."

"Yeah."

"Do you think she'll bring you something? Like a diamond necklace? Or something?"

"Dunno. Probably. But my aunt's going bananas. The visit's wrecking our holidays."

"Where were you going?"

"Grand Coulee Dam. The Eighth Wonder of the World."

"Holy."

"Yeah. All that water."

NINETEEN

Billy

Billy and his bi-weekly visits. When he was with us it was as if some marvellous deity had taken up residence. Several days before there'd be the quiet pleasure of seeing him soon and then, as the Friday night neared, the full-blown anticipation of his arrival, an event as certain to me as a law of nature, as reliable as the phases of the moon or the changing tides. You could chart your movements, or your life, by the surety of Billy's visits.

There were preparations, certainly, though nothing overt: his sheets on the downstairs cot would be washed, his favourite foods bought – Cheezies, tinned spaghetti, cheddar cheese, sliced bologna. And Elsie would get a warning tone in her voice: "Billy's coming. Clean up that bloody mess in your bedroom."

Then he would be with us. His grip tossed nonchalantly by the front door. His jacket flung over the back of a chair. He'd stay until the seven ferry on Sunday night. Between those times he gave Elsie money for the Saturday night steaks and the Sunday night roast beef. He handed out my allowance, two one-dollar bills meant to last two weeks, and took me shopping for any store-bought clothes I might need, or shoes, or school supplies. And on the first Friday night of every month he gave Elsie a fifty-dollar bill for my room and board.

His job during these weekend visits was simple: to adore me, to praise to the heavens all that I did, and to enthusiastically encourage all that I wished to do. My job was to never disappoint him or make him ashamed of me, never hurt his feelings, never neglect him, and always laugh at his jokes.

THE BUS FROM THE ferry was dropping Billy off at the end of Cordova Bay Road. I had driven up there with Ernie to pick him up, and I watched closely as he hopped from the bus and strode towards the car. How was he taking the news about Nancy? I was looking for signs of distress. He had on his weekend summer clothes, the beige straw hat, his blue open-necked shirt, the light-grey pants. But he acted like always – jaunty, swinging his grip, happy to see us.

"Hallo-allo-allo," he said, getting into the back seat. "How's ducks?" He smiled at me. "You look like you've had some sun!"

He lit up a cigarette. Rothmans filter. And snapped the Zippo lighter shut.

Ernie was already puffing away on a cigarette; his neck was shiny with sweat. "It's going to be a hot one for the holiday," he said miserably. "Weatherman's calling for ninety degrees tomorrow. Going to be stifling in the library."

"But surely the library's not open on Dominion Day?" Billy said.

"It is for me," Ernie grumbled. "Got to go in and check on the boilers first thing. Check and make sure they're turned off."

"But you won't be there all day?"

"No. But it'll be stifling in the library."

"I bet it will be," Billy said, winking at me. "Those books could do with a swim."

I groaned.

"Hah! That's a good one," Ernie said.

It was like this all the way home. Annoyingly chit-chatty. Jokey. When we pulled into the driveway, Billy grinned at me and said, "I have to get a haircut this weekend. Matter of fact, think I'll get them all cut."

Ernie's shoulders moved up and down. "Heh, heh." As if he hadn't heard the joke a million times. I forced a laugh because Billy was expecting it.

"I had to get my boils lanced," I blurted out, trying for a more sober mood in light of Nancy's threatened visit. "There was a bucket of pus."

"So Elsie told me. That must have been some procedure."

"When did she tell you that?"

"On the phone this afternoon."

"Oh."

That night I listened at my bedroom door as I always did on the Friday nights when Billy was over. (In this case it was a Thursday.) Elsie and Billy were sitting at the kitchen table with a pot of tea between them. It was late, past ten; Ernie had gone to bed. I could hear Rip's leg banging the floor scratching fleas and then Elsie shouted, "Stop that!" And dragged him outside to his doghouse.

Friday night reports were a ritual. Elsie talked, Billy listened. The subject was always the same – what had gone on with me during Billy's two-week absence. During these talks I became this other girl called She or Her, a girl who starred in Elsie's telling but who often failed in the endearing department: She or Her was a demanding and defiant girl whose sole purpose in life was to aggravate her aunt. No wonder I loved the Tom Sawyer and Huckleberry Finn books. Tom and Huck were motherless, too, but what wonderful lives they were having anyway.

And they were crafty-smart, independent, and lovable in spite of what Tom's aunt or Huck's father thought.

I strained at my door to hear what Elsie and Billy were saying. I wanted details about Nancy's visit. Why? For how long? Where *will* she sleep? This question scared me. "We've no room here!" I wanted to make sure they understood this. "She can't stay here!"

And I wanted to know how Billy was taking it. But Elsie was going on about my boils. From her voice I could picture her face: pinched and offended. "We had to hold her down in Dr. Bryant's office," she was saying. "You wouldn't have believed the fuss. Hollering. Screaming. Carrying on. I was so embarrassed."

Billy mumbled something; he spoke so softly.

"On a rock. She scraped it swimming way out at Seal Rock. Even after I've told her she's not to go that far. But she never listens to me. She does what she likes. She's got a mind of her own. And look what happens! A staph infection! Penicillin! And you know what that costs!"

Suddenly I was deeply upset. Hadn't Elsie held my hand in Dr. Bryant's office? Hadn't she acted nice for a change and bought me a comic when we'd left the doctor's office?

I burst through the door. "That's not true," I screamed. "I didn't make a big fuss! It hurt. You've changed everything. Just like you always do. You're always making things up."

They both stared at me over their teacups. Billy looked guilty.

Then Elsie said, annoyed, "Listening at doors!" She turned to Billy. "See what I have to put up with?"

I slammed my door so hard the bedroom window shook and Rip started barking.

Ernie came charging up from downstairs. "What the heck?" I heard him say. "I thought it was an earthquake."

THE NEXT MORNING, JULY 1, I was travelling in the car with Billy to Smith's store to buy pop for the holiday supper. He'd just given me five dollars in a letter that began, "The Bored of Education is so pleased you passed grade seven ..."

The way he'd made a pun of the word "Board" – I was supposed to laugh. Instead, I gave him a weak smile. "Thanks for the money." I was feeling miserable. Elsie hadn't spoken to me at breakfast. I was getting the silent treatment, something usually reserved for Ernie.

We were driving along. Billy cleared his throat several times before he finally spoke. "Your mother wants to see you. That's why she's coming."

I shrank, alarmed. This was the first-ever time he'd mentioned Nancy to me outright. Was I now going to witness his heart breaking all over again? Here in the car, driving along through the otherwise-sunny day? "What for?" I managed to say. "What does she want to see me for?"

"She says she got an odd thank-you letter from you," Billy continued with pursed lips, his fingers tapping the steering wheel. I could tell he hated this talk as much as I did. "Something about your strange writing. Do you know anything about this?"

"No," I said, remembering in panic *Wiss Warion Gibson* and the thank-you letter I'd written.

"She's worried about you."

"Worried? That's a good one."

Billy hesitated. "Maybe you should be seeing more of your mother. Now that you're getting older. Get to know her. And the way you and Elsie fight ..."

"No!"

"But shouldn't a girl be with her mother?"

Not this mother, I wailed inwardly. Instead, I said, "You mean live in Australia? Leave Rip and all my friends?"

"Well ..."

"And Maudie and Grandma? And Doreen and Bob? And Ernie and ... *you*?" There, I'd finally said it ... sort of: *I'd never leave you.*

"Well ..."

"And Elsie? And the beach? And the Point? And Miss Blythe and ..."

"Hold on, hold on," Billy said, smiling now. "You don't have to go off the deep end. It's just," he stammered, "if you could be a little nicer to Elsie. It's not easy for her either. What with everything that's going on."

"What? What's going on?"

"Well, the change of life ..."

"The what?"

Billy looked away. Then he said, "I know! Why don't we kick up our heels on Saturday afternoon and see a movie? Eh? What do you say? That new Doris Day movie at the Odeon about eating daisies. How 'bout it?"

"Okay," I said. Reluctantly. Because I'd planned to be at the beach on Saturday afternoon, and because Doris Day was a dipstick. "But I'm not moving to Australia. I'm not leaving Cordova Bay."

"No," Billy said. "No."

"And I'll be nicer to Elsie. I'll try."

"Now you're cooking with gas."

But he looked so sad. He glanced at me. "I won't be here when your mother visits. I'll be busy in Vancouver."

I didn't say anything. My throat was burning; I couldn't bear to be the cause of his unhappiness. I turned and looked out the window so he wouldn't see me cry.

[TWENTY]

Nancy and Billy

It wasn't that I hated Nancy. It was more compli- cated than that. Memories, for starters. In spite of my best efforts, they'd surface whenever her orbit neared mine. I had a list of memories, and they were mostly bad ones: the times she left me with strangers, sometimes for days; her impulsive anger, the sudden slaps across my face if I interrupted her with a question, if I'd wet the bed, had not eaten my supper; the time in Vancouver when she threw a bowl of gravy at Billy and it smashed against the kitchen wall – brown gravy, white wall; the constant daily betrayals, often over the smallest things – a walk not taken, a story not read. I'd stopped looking to the adults around me for explanations, but I did want answers: Why was she like that? I wanted not to feel so different because of her, not be reminded that I was a girl without a mother, a girl whose mother was willingly absent.

When I was six Billy had sent her money. To come back to us, Elsie told me later, to make of us a proper family. I was playing in the lane across from the Cordova Bay house when Doreen and Shirley found me one Saturday morning. They ran towards me, laughing with excitement. "You've got to come home! Your mother's coming this afternoon!" I didn't share their excitement, though; I felt only a curious flatness, a reluctance to join in their merriment. Nancy was coming "out of the blue," they said. "Isn't it wonderful?"

Elsie took charge as she always did. My hair was washed and curled, my best clothes ironed. I submitted to these preparations, but I could not participate in everyone's apparent enjoyment. Just as well, as it turned out. Nancy didn't arrive as scheduled. When it became obvious she wasn't coming at all, everyone looked at me sadly and said, "Oh, you poor thing." Sometime later, Elsie discovered the truth from Billy. "Nancy used the money to buy a mink coat," she declared, scandalized. "She chose a mink coat over a daughter!" But I was hugely relieved: maybe this meant the end of Nancy.

DURING MY FIRST YEARS with Elsie I'd had a recurring nightmare. It was this: I'm a small child in a foreign country and I've stolen a cookie from a shop, a cream cookie, hexagonal in shape. It fits in the palm of my hand. I steal this cookie and flee in panic through heavy traffic; angry shopkeepers are chasing me. Suddenly a winged angel appears and lifts me by the shoulders, like a rabbit plucked from the ground by an eagle. Together we soar over city streets, and then countryside, and then a vast ocean, arriving in an instant at the Cordova Bay house, where I am dropped in the driveway. This most unexpected place, my future home, is quietly beautiful, with mown lawns and flower gardens, the sea bright as a mirror beyond. But it's a nightmare because the female angel is impersonal and efficient, without a face. She's swift as a darting bird and she simply drops me – a foundling, the eternally abandoned baby – and then carries on. Perhaps if the angel had spoken, shown some warmth and reassurance, I might not have felt so afraid. But she did none of these things. My rescuer never speaks.

There were three good memories of Nancy, the first two involving cruise ships in the South Pacific.

Good memory #1: I threw my coat overboard and Nancy made the captain stop the boat while a crew member retrieved it with a long pole. That night, dining at the captain's table, Nancy laughed loudly, delightedly, "What a naughty little girl you are!" I was five.

Good memory #2: We missed the boat. This was in Suva, Fiji. We were in the back seat of a taxi with a man in a white suit, a man named Jerry. I could see the ship steaming away from the dock, getting smaller and smaller in the distance. Nancy was screaming, "Oh God! Oh God!" Then we were in a speedboat racing towards the ship and Jerry was left on shore waving. The ship stopped and a metal stair was let down. I was three years old and frightened of the heaving sea, of climbing the swaying stair. Nancy carried me. "There, there," she said warmly, kissing my hair.

Good memory #3: I was sitting beside my mother while she played the piano for a group of people. A party somewhere in Australia; I was four or five. People with drinks in their hands were crowded around the piano singing. When Nancy finished a tune they would call out, "Play us another one, Nancy. Play 'Kitten on the Keys.' Play 'The Happy Wanderer.' Play 'My Love Is like a Red, Red Rose.'" I was at the centre of this happy, singing world, pounding on the shrill high notes at the end of the piano, the ones that are never used. Nancy turned to me between songs and asked, "What shall we play next, darling?" Darling! The music of that rare caress!

Still, these good memories were not enough. If I could have shopped at a special department store that sold mothers, I would not have chosen Nancy. I'd have chosen Margaret on *Father Knows Best*, or Doreen, or, in a pinch, Mrs. Holt next door. Having Nancy as a mother was like a price I had to pay for being loved by Billy and Elsie and the rest of the family. And now "Your mother's coming!" was, once again, like a warning or a threat. Or a perverse reminder to me that the flip side of all the good things I had in my life was the shadow of Nancy and what she represented: my essential lack.

When I was eight I had taken a pencil to a picture in Maudie's photo album, a picture of Nancy and Billy. They're dressed up and sitting at a table – it looks as if they're at a dance. Nancy has a flower in her hair and a full glass of beer before her. I'd been idly flipping through the album when I came across this picture. It may have been just after Christmas when, again, a present had not arrived from her. I grabbed a nearby pencil and scratched lines across Nancy's face. From then on I refused to call her Mother; I would only call her by her first name. The word "mother" sat hard and bitter in my throat.

But I wasn't going to think about any of this now. I was going to be put out, inconvenienced by her impending visit. I was going to be irritated. I looked up the word in the dictionary: irritate – *to make annoyed or angry.*

"What a royal pain," I told myself repeatedly. "What a royal bloody *irritating* pain."

TWENTY-ONE

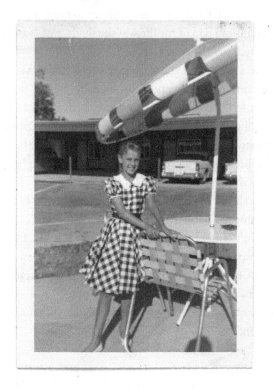

Marion

Elsie worked in the kitchen on the morning of Dominion Day making pies. By noon everything except the ham was ready. The three finished pies – cherry, apple, and raisin – sat side by side on the kitchen table like competing pies at a country fair. Also on the table were two bowls of potato chips, one of smooth, one of crinkled; an empty cut-glass bowl for the onion chip dip, which was being kept in the fridge; a bowl of Cheezies, because Billy loved them; a dish of bread-and-butter pickles, because Doreen loved these; and a large bowl containing two dozen white buns – Parker House rolls – still in their plastic bags. Eight turquoise plastic plates, brought out from the china cabinet in the living room, were stacked on the table beside four everyday white plates, twelve knives and forks, and a stack of white paper napkins. Besides the plates and cutlery, there was a Peter Rabbit bowl for Lyn and a pair of fat salt and pepper shakers, turquoise-and-black in colour, garden gnome in design. The special tablecloth – white plastic, thin as tissue paper – had a faint design of pink and yellow umbrellas. There were flowers in the centre of the table, too, red tulips, also plastic; the teapot, cream jug, sugar bowl, and cups and saucers were placed neatly to one side. The ham, now in the oven, had been spread with a gooey mixture of hot-dog mustard and maple syrup and covered with a tinfoil tent.

All this preparation, and it was only noon. Would the day never begin? There were four or five hours to go until we could actually eat the chips and the pickles, and eventually the sliced ham, along with the potato salad that Maudie was bringing and the bean salad that Doreen was bringing. Until then we were free to wander in and out of the kitchen, where we could sniff the baking ham and admire the food and the dishes on the table. They'd been arranged, I thought, to look like a photo display in the *Star Weekly* or in my home-ec textbook, where in a picture a tall, smiling, blond woman wearing a frilly apron and high heels was placing a platter of food on a decorated table. The caption beneath read: *Celebrate the Holidays with a Special Meal!*

Because our small kitchen table was full, we ate lunch in the den off TV trays, nothing fancy, just hurried salmon sandwiches and tea because Elsie was too busy to do more, she said; she still had the kitchen floor to wash.

While the four of us were eating Ernie said, "Why are you bothering to wash and wax the kitchen floor? No one will even go in there."

Elsie took this as criticism and stiffened. "Little do you know," she said crossly.

Ernie shook his head dismissively and tut-tutted. He acted bolder when Billy was around. He put down his sandwich and hauled a hand-kerchief out of his back pocket. He sighed and made a big deal of cleaning his glasses. I looked at Elsie and thought of cartoons, the ones where smoke comes out of people's ears to indicate seething anger. She looked like that, like she might explode. But no one was laughing.

Here we go, I thought. As usual everything had changed in a heart-beat. The air had become charged and menacing; the land mines were in place. "See what I have to put up with," I wanted to tell Billy.

But he seemed oblivious to all of this. He sat on the other end of the couch from me with his socked feet curled beneath him, a sandwich in one hand, holding the *TV Guide* with the other.

Ernie had finished with his glasses and resumed eating when I noticed with alarm that he had a hunk of white bread stuck to the corner of his mouth. I worried that Elsie would see it and say, "Wipe your bloody mouth," and Ernie would spit back, "Wipe your own bloody mouth!" and then the July first supper with the perfectly laid table and the ham and the pies and everyone coming would be ruined.

But they didn't explode, not this time; everything stayed nice and smouldering. Actually, I preferred an explosion. That cleared the air and guaranteed at least a week of silence between them, even though the silence was hostile; they wouldn't speak or even acknowledge one another's existence. But this state was preferable to living through a gathering storm when you were edgy with the waiting. Best, of course, was make-up day, when it was as if the windows had suddenly burst open and the house was flooded with warm yellow light. On such a day either of them might declare, "What the heck! So what if it's Tuesday? Let's kick up our heels and go out for fish and chips!"

But we hadn't had a make-up day since Christmas.

Billy took a long, slurpy sip of tea – "Ah! That hits the spot!" – then turned to Ernie and me. "Want to come get Maudie and Grandma? Go for a drive first? Get an ice cream? We'll get out of Elsie's hair. Give her a chance to get things shipshape."

We left at one thirty, when Elsie was on her hands and knees with a pail of water, grimly scrubbing the kitchen floor. Billy drove (it was, after all, his car). Ernie was in the passenger's seat, and I was in the back. We went along for a while but nobody spoke. It was a bright day. Earlier, Elsie had worried about the high white haze that was threatening to cover the sun and spoil the supper, but it was fine now and hot; everything was fine. I was wearing my new turquoise shorts; my sweaty legs stuck to the vinyl car seat.

Along Blenkinsop Road, through farmland dotted with grazing cows and with the hot sun baking the inside of the car, I yelled, "Let's open all the windows!" Which Billy and Ernie did, a blast of hot air hitting our faces. They were wearing identical baseball hats – white with blue visors – so the fringe around their bald heads didn't blow. But my hair did when I untied my ponytail and let the wind slap strands of hair into my mouth.

Billy hollered above the wind and the engine noise, "Isn't this the life?" and Ernie actually smiled and turned around and handed me a hard candy, lime, my favourite.

We drove along the Victoria waterfront, and then through Beacon Hill Park, and watched people feeding ducks there from plastic bags full of bread. We drove the loop of Clover Point, where the sea was sparkling blue and silver and people were flying kites on the grass by the parking lot. We stopped for soft ice cream cones at the Beacon Drive-In, all our cones large size and dipped in hot milk chocolate; we were still hungry from lunch.

I wasn't thinking about Nancy's visit. She didn't enter my head even once.

NEAR THREE O'CLOCK WE were on the hill at the top of Maudie's street and could see Grandma standing at the end of their driveway waiting for us.

"Would you look at that!" Billy laughed. "I wonder how long she's been waiting."

Even though it was ninety degrees out, Grandma had on her black coat and hat. Her heavy black purse was hanging off her good arm; she only had a sock-covered stump for her right hand, because years ago it had been amputated after a fall. The stump waved at us impatiently.

When she climbed into the back seat beside me she said, "About time."

Billy looked at his watch and shouted. "We're early, Ma. It's not even three."

"You're late," she shouted back. "Why can't you ever be on time? I've been waiting for over an hour. And now I've missed the parade."

Billy and Ernie looked at each other and rolled their eyes.

Maudie came hurrying out of the house carrying the bowl of potato salad, which was covered with several layers of plastic wrap. "Cripes!" she laughed, handing me the bowl. "I don't think I locked the back door!" And hurried towards the back of the house.

Ernie hung his head out the car window and called, "What do you want to lock all the doors for? Kenny's still in bed. Afraid someone will steal him?"

Billy snorted.

"Lazy bugger," said Ernie.

Grandma said, "Eh?"

"Kenny's a lazy bugger!" I shouted.

"I know that," Grandma said. "You don't have to shout!"

Maudie hadn't heard any of this. When she returned to the car she was laughing; she bounced up and down on the car seat as we drove towards the Bay.

[TWENTY-TWO]

Bob

When we got home four cars, including Ernie's truck, were parked in the driveway. Right away Ernie got peeved. He liked to direct traffic. He liked to make people park their cars where he told them. What if there were an emergency? What if someone had to leave in a hurry?

In the carport and adjoining patio on the street side of the house, he'd set up wooden deck chairs and several kitchen chairs and now most of these were filled. Everyone had to sit facing the badly parked cars and, beyond, the traffic of Cordova Bay Road, because it was too windy on the other side of the house, the side with the sea view and the new brick barbecue. Grandma hated the wind, and if we'd sat facing the ocean, she'd have stubbornly stayed in the carport by herself.

The Old Martyr was what Ernie called her most of the time. "She'd cut off her nose to spite her face."

His own family – two sisters, Mildred and Dotsy, who had loud English voices, and a bent old father, who lived in the Home – hardly ever visited, let alone came to our family suppers. Which was fine by Elsie. She had a story about them, naturally. After hearing it many times I called it "Turkish Delight."

His family never liked me. Right from the start. A widow with two girls. They never got over my marrying Ernie after Sonny died. Ernie was thirty-nine years old and still lived at home with his mother and father. He had a steady job at the library and paid all their bills. His mother and his sisters thought he'd go on giving them money like before but all that changed when he married me. So that was strike number one. Strike number two was the boxes of Purdy's chocolates that Ernie used to buy them every week. That stopped, too. Big expensive boxes of chocolates. I've never seen women eat chocolates like they did! And their mother, too, when she was alive. They could go through a box of Purdy's in an hour, all of them hanging over the box, picking out the creams. If they bit into a Turkish delight, which they hated, they'd scream and give it to the dog. No wonder they were all so fat. Strike three was my strike – I gave up trying to get along with Ernie's family, trying to get them to like me. At Christmas I'd give his mother and sisters bars of fancy soap because they wore perfume that was so strong it made you choke. I thought the soaps would be something different for them. But they never said thank you so I don't give them presents anymore. Now it's just a card.

Bob came out of the house carrying a cooler full of beer and Orange

Crush. Predictably, he grinned at me and said, "Hi Sexy!" And then, "Heard Auntie Nancy's coming for a visit. There'll be a hot time in the old town tonight," he chuckled.

"Shut up. You don't even know her."

"But I will, won't I? Now I'll finally get to meet your famous mother. Can't wait to get the old gal around the piano."

"Just shut up."

"Ooooo. Hi Sexy's in a bad mood," Bob said, making his voice go shrill like a girl's. "I'm so scared."

Doreen came out the door squealing, "Oh, Marion! Isn't it something! Now we're really going to have some fun. I wonder what Auntie Nancy's wearing these days. Probably something fabulous. I can't wait to see her!"

"Shush," I snarled, anxious that Billy might hear.

But he was in the kitchen talking with Elsie.

Grandma was seated on a kitchen chair under the shade of the carport roof and announced crankily to no one in particular, "It's terrible to get old. Everything hurts. And I'm always cold. There's always a draft."

"There's no draft today," someone hollered. "It's nearly a hundred degrees out. Aren't you hot in that coat?

"Eh?"

"AREN'T YOU HOT, WEARING A COAT?"

"Eh?"

"GOT YOUR HEARING AID TURNED OFF?"

"Eh?"

The baby, Lyn, wearing a turquoise sunsuit, had recently learned to walk and was moving unsteadily from chair to chair. When she got to Grandma, she grabbed the strap of the purse that Grandma held firmly on her lap in case someone tried to steal it. "Oh, no you don't," Grandma yelled. They had a tug-of-war for a while that Lyn lost, finally flopping to the ground and howling with rage. Maudie hurried over and picked her up. Then walked around with her, bouncing her up and down, singing, "I'm a little teapot, short and stout ..."

There were three guests at the Dominion Day supper who were not related to us: old Mrs. Bland, who owned a cottage farther down the beach and spent the summers there by herself, and Fred and Marge, friends of Elsie and Ernie's, who lived in a trailer up-Island. "As man and wife," Elsie said, but they were not actually married: *Marge was a slave to her husband and his parents until one day she just upped and left. When she took up with Fred, it was a scandal. His company shipped him off to Port Alberni.*

Marge and Fred, middle-aged and impeccably dressed, sat quietly side by side on deck chairs in the sun and spoke little.

While Grandma and the baby had been tussling over the purse, Marge and Fred and Mrs. Bland had looked on with blank faces.

"Lovely day," Mrs. Bland finally said when the episode was over, waving her cane at a wasp.

"Umm," said Marge and Fred politely. They each wore a wedding ring.

I'd recently had a conversation with Elsie about them.

Me: "It's so fake. Wearing wedding rings. Pretending to be married when you're not."

Elsie: "It's because people in Port Alberni don't know the truth. If they did Fred would lose his job."

Me: "Why don't they just get married?"

Elsie: "They can't. Fred's wife and Marge's husband won't give them a divorce."

Me: "So they did it for love? They ran away for love?"

Elsie: "More like burned their bridges. Marge's kids won't have anything to do with her now. We're their only friends."

I took a special interest in Marge and Fred because they had notoriety like Nancy did, even if theirs was of a milder variety. With Marge and Fred, though, I never got beyond the business of "running away for love," because I couldn't reconcile this act with the two unattractive people sitting so stiffly on our patio. If you ran away for love you had to be handsome or beautiful, or at the very least young, and Marge and Fred were none of these things. Fred was a large, fleshy man with a double chin and a wide stomach; Marge was tall and thin with a pinched mouth and a large nose. They weren't very friendly, either, but coolly formal. I could imagine Nancy "running away for love" – no need to imagine because she'd reputedly done it many times – but not this sour old couple.

AT FOUR THIRTY KENNY pulled into the driveway.

"Here comes Elvis the Pelvis," Bob said, looking around for laughs, making do with a few smirks. He was sitting on the low concrete front step, a cigarette in one hand, a bottle of beer in the other.

"All he does is sleep. Won't even take out the garbage. Maudie has to." This was from Grandma. She was so short she could swing her legs while she sat.

Maudie beamed at the sight of Kenny's car and leaped up in an ecstasy of admiration for her only child. "He's here!" she announced, laughing, breathless. "He made it!"

Kenny's hot rod was lowered at the front to eight inches off the ground. It was a dark-green 1946 Mercury Coupe with fuzzy dice hanging from the rear-view mirror and fuzzy white balls lining the inside around the windshield; the muffler was shot.

The engine roared – "vroom, vroom" – even while idling in the driveway. From behind, Kenny's hot rod looked rude, with its rear end poking high into the air, like a car that was sticking out its tongue and taunting, "Nya nya nya."

Kenny sounded the horn and waved. It was a trick horn that played a selection of recognizable tunes. This time it played the first notes of "The Yellow Rose of Texas." Excited, I ran to meet him. Ernie was hot behind me, puffing; at last he'd get to direct traffic.

"Park it over there," he called seriously. "Beside the fence."

Kenny let me carry his case of beer to the house. He carried his guitar himself. His cigs, as he called them, were tucked into the rolled-up sleeve of his white T-shirt.

"Afternoon, ladies," he said in his Elvis voice when he reached the carport.

The "ladies," including his mother but not Grandma, who pointedly looked the other way, inclined their heads and smiled. It surprised me the way they acted so dainty when Kenny with his Elvis manners was around – genteel, as if they were in a movie about the Old South – sipping lemonade, fanning themselves in the heat, fragile, cosseted, helpless women.

Ernie, meanwhile, was busily shoving wire hoops into the tiny grassed area next to the patio in case anyone wanted to play croquet later on.

By late afternoon we were still sitting outside watching the traffic, or the baby, and waiting for supper. I'd made Rip do tricks for everyone – sit up, roll over – and had thrown a lacrosse ball back and forth with Billy. No one was interested in playing croquet. "Too hot!" everyone groaned, feigning heat exhaustion.

At one point Kenny strummed his guitar, singing quietly, "Pack up all your cares and woe ..." And, "Oh, we ain't got a barrel of money, maybe we're ragged and funny ..." Only Maudie, Doreen, and I sang along; Marge and Fred looked away, embarrassed.

Just before supper Bob started goofing around in his bathing suit, adding gumboots and a cowboy hat, pretending to be a cowboy: "Whaddya say, pardner?" He pointed one of my old cap guns at Doreen, the baby, me. I took his picture with my Brownie camera.

"Oh, Bob. Grow up," Doreen said languidly from a deck chair where she was spreading oil on her long tanned legs. "You're nearly thirty. Quit acting like a kid."

She looked like one of the pinups on Kenny's calendars – stunningly attractive in her white shorts and yellow halter top. She was so beautiful to look at that sometimes I would stand and stare at her, trying to absorb her beauty like heat from a lamp, trying to understand where such beauty came from.

THE DOMINION DAY SUPPER came to a weary end; it was suddenly boring, massively, time-made-of-cement boring. After dessert everyone still sat on the carport patio, Marge and Fred quietly smoking, their cigarettes poised at the edge of the huge ashtray on a stand that had been brought outside especially for them; the men and Doreen listlessly drinking from bottles of beer, the others, cups of tea. A slight wind had come up, and we watched a paper napkin flit across the grass and lodge at the base of a croquet hoop. Cars moved in a thick, slow line along Cordova Bay Road. How much longer could we go on watching the traffic, or the baby? Or saying dull things to each other. "Nice day." "Nice pie." The whole dinner, begun at five, was over by a quarter to six. Now what? I wanted to call up Doris and tear down to the beach.

Then Grandma yelled towards the men, "What're you drinking that muck for?" initiating her usual game of pouring full bottles of beer down the sink. Everyone routinely laughed when she did this – it was one of the things that now made her a "character" – and made a show of hiding their bottles. Last Dominion Day Bob had stapled her black straw hat to the carport roof.

"Eh?" Kenny now said on cue.

"It's good for our health," Bob added, half-heartedly.

At quarter to seven Grandma and Maudie struggled into Kenny's car for the ride home. There was no back seat, so the three of them sat tilted forward in the front, Grandma in the middle, her black hat barely visible above the dashboard. Kenny revved the engine three or four times and Maudie leaned out the car window laughing and waving a white handkerchief at us as if she were going on a world cruise. Kenny sounded the horn; this time it was the first notes of "She'll Be Coming 'Round the Mountain." Suddenly they took off in a flurry of dust and flung gravel. The tires squealed when they hit Cordova Bay Road, turning left for town. Then they were gone. We could hear the "vroom, vroom" of the hot rod for a few moments after they were out of sight.

TWENTY-THREE

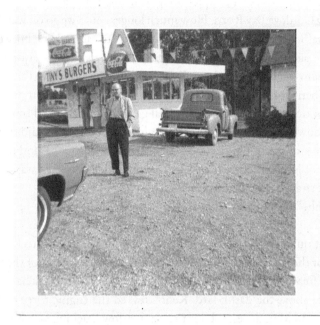

Ernie

There were thirteen days now until Nancy's visit.

It was a countdown: thirteen, twelve, eleven ...

Here was the plan. Nancy was flying into the Victoria airport at eleven in the morning on July 14. Elsie, Ernie, and I would meet her in the Zephyr, bring her to Cordova Bay for lunch, and then take her to Maudie's house, where she'd have Grandma's old room with the single bed. No one knew if Nancy was bringing a new husband, but if she was, he would sleep on a cot in Kenny's room. On the day of her arrival we'd have a special supper at Maudie's – roast beef, Yorkshire pudding, apple pie. Doreen and Bob and Lyn would be there, and Kenny, who would probably be up by then. Our trip to Grand Coulee Dam, the Eighth Wonder of the World, in Washington state, was cancelled. Instead, Ernie would be available to chauffeur Nancy and the rest of us around. Billy, of course, wouldn't show his face.

Grandma had forgotten she hated Nancy. "Who's coming?" she kept saying. "Never heard of her."

No one knew how long Nancy was staying.

ON DAY TEN TO NANCY'S visit I came home from a morning spent on the beach with Doris wading between the double sandbars searching for crabs. I found Doreen and Elsie sitting at the kitchen table and Lyn on the kitchen floor hauling pots and lids out of the cupboard.

Elsie was crying.

"What happened?" I thought Grandma had died. I put my pail on the countertop; it held a large Dungeness crab that I'd planned to cook up and have with bread and butter for lunch.

"Nothing," Elsie sobbed.

I stood there, rubbing sand from my bare feet with my toes.

"You might as well tell her," Doreen said quietly. "She'll find out soon enough."

"What?"

But Elsie kept on crying. She had a dishtowel held to her face and her glasses were off. It scared me to see her like this – broken, vulnerable. Doreen was sitting beside her, an arm around her shoulder. She explained. "Mom had a phone call from Auntie Mildred."

My heart was pounding.

"Pop's seeing another woman."

"Another woman?"

Doreen nodded. "Mrs. Johns. The lady he gives a ride into work every morning. She works at Evelyn's Café, the coffee shop beside the library. Pop took her to Auntie Mildred's for tea."

"Oh, I can just see Mildred's face!" Elsie wailed through the dish-towel. "She's loving every minute of this, I know it. The satisfaction it must be giving her! Phoning me up. Rubbing my nose in it."

"Ernie and another woman?" I asked, incredulous. The thought of him "running away for love" like Marge and Fred had done was beyond belief. I couldn't picture him away from his chocolate bars, the TV set, the Three Stooges.

"And it's not the first time he's taken her to his sister's for tea," Elsie continued. "Apparently he's done it before. Must have taken time off work. Oh, it makes me sick thinking about it. All those tarts and cookies Mildred would have made especially and put out on her fancy plates. For Ernie and Mrs. Johns! It pierces me to the bone! Mildred said he even had on his best clothes. Must have snuck them out of the house and kept them at work. His grey flannel pants and his navy-blue blazer that I've just had cleaned." Here she let out a deep sob before continuing. "Mildred *had* to add that about his best clothes. She would. Oh, the humiliation! She's probably still laughing about it now, telling everyone she knows, enjoying every minute of this. And on top of everything else. What with Nancy coming! And our holidays ruined! Oh, that Mildred. I could just spit at her!"

"I knew you should never have married Pop," Doreen said. "Didn't I tell you?" She turned to me. "I wouldn't go to the wedding. I refused. I stayed at a girlfriend's house."

"That's right," Elsie said, nodding her head mournfully. "Shirley came, but you wouldn't."

"Shirley was ten and didn't know any better. I was fourteen. But Pop's family never liked us, did they? They were always mean to us. Weren't they mean? When you first married Pop?"

"They didn't even get new clothes for the wedding," Elsie said, dabbing her eyes. "And Maudie and Ma had to do all the work, making the sandwiches and the wedding cake. The Sextons didn't lift a bloody finger. I felt like Cinderella with the ugly stepsisters."

We laughed, sort of.

"What does she look like? Mrs. Johns?" I asked. "Is she beautiful or icky?"

"I've never laid eyes on the woman," Elsie sniffed. "For all I know she's colour-blind, walks on her hands, and spits wooden nickels."

Doreen hooted.

"But I do know," Elsie continued, "that she's got a husband and a son and lives in that plain house on the corner."

"We should go spy on her," Doreen said, deliciously. "We should hop in the car this very minute and go to Evelyn's Café and see what this Mrs. Johns looks like."

"Yeah," I said, excited by the adventure.

"Or phone up Mr. Johns and tell him what's going on," Doreen added. "See what he thinks about that!"

"No. Let's go to Evelyn's Café!" I urged. "We'll sit at the counter and order Cokes and fries. Or a chocolate milkshake. And spy on her. And see what she does." This was so thrilling, like being a detective, a real one. Already I was deciding what to take along: notebook, magnifying glass, my Brownie camera ...

Elsie ignored me. "I can't believe Ernie would take up with another woman," she said, sobbing anew. "You'd think he was some kind of Romeo."

"A fat, bald Romeo," Doreen said.

"A stinky Romeo," I added.

Elsie shrieked. "Marion! That's an awful thing to say!"

"Well. You said so yourself."

"It's true," she said, turning to Doreen. "When I first married Ernie I had to get him to take regular baths. He hadn't been trained to keep himself clean."

"I know, Mom," Doreen sighed. "He smelled."

I was sitting at the kitchen table with them by now, loving the fact that I was in on everything. We said nothing for a few moments. I started thinking about Ernie, the way he was like smoke about the house, so indistinct and ill-defined, always in the background – there, in his recliner chair before the TV set; at the supper table, silent over his meal; alone in his workshop, sawing, hammering. At home I barely noticed him; it was Elsie's life and my life that we seemed to be living. Ernie was a bit player, a man with a minor supporting role. It was unimaginable that he could be someone else – a man seeing another woman. Wasn't he the butt of Elsie's complaints, the person who slipped out of the house in the dark with his lunch pail each morning, the person whose refrain from the sidelines was always "Nag, nag"? It was hard to think of him as separate and distinct, as a person in his own right, whole, fully formed – a man with *a mind of his own.*

The best time I had with him was watching *Fun-O-Rama* in the afternoons. Once we'd laughed so hard at Mighty Mouse pretending to be an opera singer underwater that Rip had started barking. Mighty Mouse sang his theme song in a soprano voice and it came out all bubbly. There was a Three Stooges episode called "Sing a Song of Six Pants" that we laughed and laughed over, too. And then I remembered all the times he'd fixed my bike, how he'd sometimes give me a quarter for candy at Smith's. I thought, too, about him sleeping in the basement since Christmas and the way Elsie bossed him around, the way they were always fighting. Suddenly I felt sorry for him. And wretched. I started to cry.

"Don't you start," Elsie said in her usual cranky voice. "I've got enough on my plate without you carrying on."

But Doreen was crying, too. "I can't help it," she bawled. "Pop's been so good to us. He's so generous and kind. He helped with the down payment on our house. He built me kitchen cabinets. He helped paint Lyn's bedroom. When Bob backed the car into that wall, Pop paid for the repairs. And what about Easter and the hot cross buns?"

The hot cross buns really sent us howling. There was Ernie in his white chef's apron standing at the kitchen table stirring the huge bowl of flour, currants, and dried fruit. He made the buns every Easter and they were delicious. He gave them to family, neighbours, the librarians at work.

"Pop's so good," Doreen cried, grabbing the dishtowel from Elsie and wiping her tears with it. "If he runs off with Mrs. Johns, what will happen to the house, to Cordova Bay? To any of us? It won't be the same without Pop."

"Hmm," Elsie said, putting on her glasses and patting her hair, getting herself straightened. "Hmm," she said again. She sat there thinking for a few moments, and then a sneaky smile crossed her face. She got up and rinsed out the teapot. She put on her apron and washed her hands.

"Well," she said at last, "that Mildred won't get the satisfaction of wrecking *my* marriage, I can tell you that."

We watched her at the sink, her arms pumping furiously as she continued scrubbing her hands. She washed them for the longest time. Bewildered, I looked at Doreen. She put a finger to her mouth: shush. I hadn't read *Macbeth* yet in school, but when I did a couple of years later, I'd think of Elsie's handwashing that day as the same thing Lady Macbeth did after the murder.

"Who does Mildred think she is, anyway?" Elsie announced at last, turning to us, defiant. There was a dangerous look on her face – her tornado look, her get-out-of-my-bloody-way look. We knew it well.

"Mildred," she snorted, untying her apron and throwing it on a chair. "Mildred. Fat bloody Mildred. With her bloody mince tarts and her bloody Florentine cookies. Thinking she can get away with giving tea to my husband and some woman. Some floozy. Well, she bloody well won't!"

"Can't we go and spy on Mrs. Johns, then?" I asked. But I knew the request was a useless one now.

"Not today," Elsie said briskly, opening the freezer at the top of the fridge and grabbing a package wrapped in brown butcher's paper. "Today we're having pork chops for supper. I'll start thawing them now."

"Pork chops? Why?" Lyn had crawled over to my chair; I picked her up.

"It's Pop's favourite supper," Doreen said, jumping up from the table, grinning through her tears. "And make a raisin pie, too," she added. "Pop loves raisin pie."

"Leave it to me," Elsie said coolly. "Leave everything to me. I'll soon put a stop to little tea parties at bloody Mildred's house."

She saw me grinning. "And you," she said fiercely, "can keep your mouth shut about any of this! Not one word. I'm warning you. Don't act any different with Ernie. You're not to let on. As far as he's concerned, it's business as usual. He won't know what hit him."

I DIDN'T KNOW WHAT was going to "hit" Ernie – what Elsie was planning – but it was all great fun. Nancy's visit paled in comparison.

I couldn't wait to tell Doris. Here was a mystery and a detective story, a real one, unfolding beneath my own roof. I didn't want to miss a thing. I was desperate to look at Ernie with fresh eyes in light of this exciting information. Already I was imagining him differently – exotic, romantic, daring – like Zorro on TV (Thursday nights at eight). Or identity-changing Superman with his love of phone booths: Ernie in the boiler room at the library swiftly changing out of his work clothes and into the debonair "taking-Mrs.-Johns-to-tea" clothes – grey flannels, navy-blue blazer. Desperately, I tried thinking of another name to call him, so I could say: *In real life he's plain old Ernie Sexton. But in his secret life he's* ... The only name I could come up with was Bookman, because he worked at the library. Still, it wasn't hard to imagine the TV show: *The Adventures of Bookman.*

I hadn't yet considered what Bookman might do other than take a middle-aged waitress to tea. But Doris had. At two thirty we were on the patio waiting for Ernie to come home from work. We wanted to see if he acted guilty, if he slunk into the house, if he looked changed in any way.

"I wonder," Doris said, giving me a sly grin, "if your uncle kisses Mrs. Johns. You know, passionately, when they're in the truck."

I both recoiled and sniggered at the thought: Ernie's purple-red fish lips puckering up to the faceless Mrs. Johns, the comedy of his bumbling ardour. And it could only be bumbling, like an episode of *The Three Stooges*. *The Adventures of Bookman* fled as a possibility.

"Why would he take her to tea unless he wanted to kiss her?" Doris continued. "Or do ... *other* things ..."

"Like what?" I cried, delighted.

"You know," Doris whispered ominously.

I did know. "You mean ... *go all the way ... do it*?"

We both groaned. Old people doing it. How icky could you get? And pathetic. And sickening.

"I'm never going to do it," I announced for about the thousandth time. "Not if you pay me a million dollars."

"Me neither," said Doris. "You know what happens if you do, don't you? Like what happened to Roberta Fraser in grade nine. My sister told me. She had to quit school and get married. She was fifteen and SHE HAD A BABY."

This, as we well knew, was the worst fate that could befall a girl.

Waiting, we could hear Elsie banging around in the kitchen. She'd been in there since lunch, making brownies, macaroons, and then the raisin pie.

"Why's your aunt making all that stuff?" Doris asked.

"Probably trying to butter up Ernie."

"Oh. You mean get in his good books?"

"Yeah. Not that he needs more cake and pie. He's fat enough."

"My mother butters up my dad when she wants more money. Buys my dad a steak. The rest of us have to eat macaroni. But the old man gets steak."

Then, the truck! Rip jumped up to greet it.

"Remember," I cautioned, "don't look at him."

"I'm scared. Isn't he going to suspect us?" Doris pleaded. "I wish we were swimming."

"Quiet!" I hissed. "Act normal. Just see if he looks guilty."

Ernie walked towards the house carrying his lunch pail. He had on the same work clothes he'd worn all week; I could see sweat stains seeping out from under his arms, and his forehead was shiny. Faced with the ordinariness of him, it was impossible to imagine him as Bookman, as being lovey-dovey in his truck with Mrs. Johns, as having secret adventures. What a dumb idea! It was plain old smelly Ernie coming towards us like always.

"Humph," he said, passing us, and went into the house. The screen door slammed behind him.

"Now what?" Doris said.

"Search me," I shrugged, disappointed. We listened a while longer, hoping Elsie and Ernie would start fighting. But it was quiet in the house. When I went inside to tell Elsie I was going to the beach – and to secretly check things out – Ernie was already in the basement, snoring away on the pullout couch.

I grinned conspiratorially at Elsie.

"What are you staring at?" she snapped. "Shouldn't you be swimming?"

TWENTY-FOUR

Doreen, Marion, Shirley

$Six days to Nancy's visit. Four since the revelation
about Mrs. Johns. Nothing to report to Doris on that front except that
we'd been eating remarkably well. And things had been eerily peaceful
between Elsie and Ernie. Quiet. Almost pleasant.

Nancy's visit now dominated everyone's life. Besides concocting
fabulous weekday meals for Ernie – Swiss steak, baked ham slices with

pineapple, and Rice-A-Roni – Elsie had been in turmoil, cleaning the house from top to bottom. Maudie and Doreen had done likewise. And everyone was baking like a maniac – cookies, squares, fruitcakes, tarts. All because of Nancy's visit.

I was affronted by this preparation. "You'd think the Queen was coming," I sniffed.

Besides the Raid that Elsie habitually sprayed around the house, she now also sprayed air freshener that came in a pretty pink-and-green can. It smelled like deodorant.

The air freshener must have given Elsie ideas, because she insulted me by presenting me with my own roll-on deodorant. "It's time," she announced bluntly. "You're beginning to smell."

"I am not!"

"You are. We'll have to start wearing gas masks if something isn't done soon."

Ernie was around when she said this, and he unaccountably winked at Elsie and grinned. To me he pinched his nose and said, predictably, "Pee-eeew!"

During the days leading up to Nancy's visit, all I heard was, "Wait till your mother gets here." And "What would your mother think?" Of me – slouching unbecomingly on the couch. Eating with my fingers. Picking my nose. Refusing to wash my hair. Wearing odd socks, and worst of all, "smelling high as a kite."

To all these accusations I'd scream, "I don't give a bloody hell what Nancy thinks!" Elsie would tut-tut indulgently and make me even madder. I did a lot of door slamming during those days before the visit.

Worst of all, though, was the morning on Day Six when Elsie decided my long hair needed cutting. She and Maudie, Grandma, and Doreen had already had their hair cut, permed, curled, and baked by Elsie's hairdresser, Rae-Ella. Now, Elsie said, it was my turn.

I cried out in alarm, "Not Godzilla! Don't make me go to Godzilla!"

"Don't call her that! How many times have I told you?"

FOR ELSIE AN IMPORTANT part of appearing well dressed was having her hair done every second Friday by a huge woman in a pink smock called Rae-Ella. Rae-Ella ran a salon that was wedged between Four Ways Market and the fish-and-chip shop. I thought the salon should have a sign out front that said "Women-Only Zone," because men were definitely not wanted there. I'd often see husbands hovering in the doorway, picking up their wives, and they looked nothing less than terrified. The salon walls were painted pink, movie magazines and coffee cups lay scattered on the tables beside the hair dryers, and the sweet, heavy scent of perfume, hairspray, and perming lotion that filled the room made your eyes water and your throat burn.

Elsie had a standing appointment with Rae-Ella at eleven every second Friday. During the summers she would drop me at Maudie's house to wait. Then I'd walk the four blocks to meet her when the appointment was over. I found Rae-Ella to be an alarming woman and a distressingly unpredictable one. Sometimes she'd be overly sweet, sweeping towards me seated on the waiting-room bench and loudly declaring, "Ah! Here's little Marion with the long blond hair! What we wouldn't give for hair like that, eh ladies?" And sometimes she was horrible and embarrassing: "A little bird told me you got a present from your mother. All the way from Australia! What was it? Lovely black-velvet shoes? A little bird told me they were three sizes too big."

"I've been going to Rae-Ella for as long as I can remember," Elsie told people, anyone. "Ever since she was a skinny blond with one chair and one hair dryer. And look what she's become today. A woman with her own business and her own car. With six chairs in her shop and two assistants. I'm her longest customer."

Over the years Rae-Ella guided Elsie's hair, which was thick and brown, through a series of permed and sprayed creations. These were styles that ranged from short to very short, depending on Elsie's and Rae-Ella's moods, the hair rising or falling on Elsie's neck like a fair-or-foul-weather barometer. Very short hair was called a pixie cut, and when she had this one, Elsie became lighthearted, even gay. For this style Rae-Ella used a special power tool, shaving Elsie's hair so far up her head that the tendons on her neck were exposed. My private name for this hairdo was The Chicken Neck.

Rae-Ella's own hair was stiff and yellow, and the style never varied; it was as tall as a wedding cake and rose magnificently on top of her head in a confection of ornate curls, often adorned with tiny pink-satin bows that looked like rosettes of cake icing. She wore bright-pink lipstick, too, and darkened a mole on her cheek in a bizarre attempt at a movie-star glamour. She was a fearsome creature, a battle-axe, as Ernie called her, catty about her workers – "a parade of useless women," she'd whisper to Elsie – and twice divorced. And because I knew that in their bi-weekly sessions Elsie told her everything about me, especially about my wandering mother and my heartbroken father, I disliked Rae-Ella immensely. Elsie was devoted to her.

I thought appointments with Rae-Ella were like going to church for Elsie. There was something sacred about the way nothing was allowed to interfere with her time in the Women-Only Zone: she and Rae-Ella cozily yakking away, the movie magazines under the dryer, the free cup of coffee, the exciting comb-out and spray, the mirror held behind Elsie's head signalling that the ritual was over. The thing I learned that I must always say to Elsie on the Friday afternoons after her appointment, and say with cheeriness and sincerity even though I didn't mean it, was, "Your hair looks nice!" Otherwise her feelings would be hurt and she'd barely speak to me. It didn't matter what her hair looked like – the half-bald pixie cut or the longer, regal, and hence more serious bouffant style – I believed I had to say this. Elsie would solemnly nod when I did so and reply with a demure "Thank you," as if it were her due.

Not only was the shape of every second Friday determined by "the Appointment," but the stories of Rae-Ella's private life dominated the supper table on Friday nights as well. We knew everything about her two marriages, and particularly the second one. This was to the man who came to fix Rae-Ella's furnace. "He took one look at the set-up," Elsie told us, "with a house all paid for and a successful business, and married her within six months."

"Poor bugger," Ernie said when he heard this.

Husband number two lasted only a year, though, because after the marriage he quit his job and lay around the house doing nothing. "Like a bum," Elsie told us with relish. "Rae-Ella soon put a stop to *that*," she added. Unlike Maudie, Rae-Ella was a slave to no man.

Then there was Rae-Ella's only daughter, the perfect Monica, who helped her mother without being asked, kept her bedroom spotless, and never talked back. Monica was my age and Elsie's yardstick, the standard against which I was frequently measured. When I was twelve and discovered that Elsie had never actually seen Monica in the flesh, but only pictures of her – "What does she look like?" "Dark-haired, plump, glasses" – I stopped paying attention.

"Rae-Ella told me Monica's learning how to knit," Elsie had said a few weeks earlier. "It's something you should do. Instead of gallivanting all over the neighbourhood."

"I don't care a fat fig about Monica. Monica's a drip."

TWENTY-FIVE

Marion

An appointment was made for me at Rae-Ella's. "Think how grown-up you'll look when your mother visits!" Elsie exclaimed. "She won't even recognize you."

"She won't recognize me anyway," I snarled. "The last time she saw me I was two feet tall."

Since I'd been actively fighting the idea of co-operating with Nancy's visit – Elsie seemed so glad to hand me over – I fought the idea of succumbing to Rae-Ella's pudgy fingers with all her scratchy diamond rings as well. But I lost. Elsie was determined. "It's time," she announced that miserable July morning. "You're thirteen years old. You're already in junior high school.

"And," she added for emphasis, "you've started developing ..."

"Don't say that word," I shrieked.

"Why not? You're going to be just like Doreen and Shirley."

"No, I'm not."

She laughed. "Oh, don't be so bloody stupid. Of course you are. You think I haven't noticed? Your undershirts have holes in the chest. They've worn right through. You'll need a brassiere soon."

"No!"

"Oh, stop it. Anyway, I've made an appointment. It's time you had a more grown-up hairdo."

"I like my ponytail," I wailed.

"That's for little girls. You're not a little girl anymore." She handed me a copy of *Silver Screen* magazine. "Here," she said, "pick out a hairstyle. See how cute Debbie Reynolds looks?"

Cute! That word again. But she knew I liked Debbie Reynolds. I had her hit record, "Tammy." Doris and I often sang it together, walking to the school bus stop, "Taaaaammy, Taaaammy, Tammy's in love ..." So I relented, charmed by Debbie Reynolds's perky blond haircut and her sweet face.

"But why does Godzilla have to cut my hair? She's an old bat and I hate her."

"I told you, don't call her that. And don't be ridiculous. How do you think it would make *me* feel if Rae-Ella found out someone else had cut your hair? I couldn't show my face."

That settled it. If I didn't go along with things I'd insult Rae-Ella and I'd humiliate Elsie. But I'd take the magazine along to the dreaded appointment to show the woman what I wanted.

RAE-ELLA HEADED TOWARDS WHERE I sat in the styling chair. I could hear her stockings rustling against her massive thighs and smell the Evening in Paris perfume she wore before she reached me. She travelled in a cloud of cloying scent.

Elsie stood nervously in the entranceway. "Take that elastic band out of your hair," she hollered, bossy.

·I glowered at her.

All around me were women in metal curlers. They grinned at me nastily. I shuddered, feeling small and alone. Were they laughing at me? I was the only girl in the salon, hopelessly young. Everyone else looked old and withered and ugly and menacing. Was my haircut, about to be performed by the majestic Rae-Ella herself, an event that was happening solely for everyone else's amusement and scorn?

Several of the women were sitting under roaring silver hairdryers that made them look like Martians with weird, elongated heads. One woman was seated at the sink with her neck stretched back in preparation for a hair wash, a neck so exposed and vulnerable it made me think of the ancient tribal sacrifices I'd read about in my social studies textbook; some weird and secret throat-slitting ritual was about to take place. Two other women were perched like crows at the counter beside me, veiny old women with tissue-paper skin who stared at me, plainly amused at my plight. Each woman had a movie magazine in her lap and a coffee cup by her side.

Brenda Lee sang smoothly from the corner radio, "I'm sorree, so sor-ree. That I wa-uz such-a fool ..."

I could see the pink scalp of the woman seated next to me. She was looking in the mirror at me while Hazel, Rae-Ella's skinny assistant (Elsie called them Mutt and Jeff), was yanking rollers from her thin white hair. Finally, the woman spoke. "Going to get it all chopped off, eh?"

"Yes," I managed to say. "Well, not all of ..."

"When I was a girl," she interrupted, "I could sit on my hair. What do you think of that?"

"Long hair's gone out of fashion," Hazel pronounced. "Better if it's short. Less work for your aunt."

The old woman smugly agreed. She had no lips.

"I can look after my own hair," I said.

Elsie heard. "Marion!"

Rae-Ella loomed beside me now. "What's this?" she said, grabbing Debbie Reynolds's picture out of my hand. She gave it a quick glance. "Wouldn't suit you," she said, tossing the picture onto the counter. "Your face is too long and your hair is too thin." She looked in the mirror for a few moments, seeming to study my head. Then she grinned broadly, as if she'd had the most brilliant idea. "I know what you need," she declared loudly. "A pixie cut!"

"No!" I turned, looking desperately for help from Elsie. But she'd stuck her face behind a movie magazine and wouldn't look up.

"What?" Rae-Ella said, startled, then softened slightly and made her voice sound like Dr. Middleton, my dentist, who was always nice before he shoved in the freezing needle. "Monica's got a pixie cut," she told me. "And Monica loves it." That settled it then. I was going to look like Monica.

She signalled to Hazel, who led me like a maiden sacrifice to the sink for the hair wash. Then, when I was seated again at the counter, my long hair dripping on the pink sheet that was tied around my neck, Rae-Ella got to work, grunting as she moved around the chair, combing and snipping, while ten-inch lengths of hair fell heavily to the floor.

I bawled all the way home.

"It's not so bad," Elsie soothed, looking worried, from the driver's seat. "I'll get out the curling iron. A little bit of curl will make all the difference."

"There's no hair left to curl," I cried. "There isn't any hair left. That stupid Godzilla cut it all off. Oh, why did you make me go there? Now I'll have to stay in the house all summer. How can I go outside looking like this?"

My hair was only three inches long in places and lay flat on my head. Spikey bits of hair hung down for bangs and jutted out on my cheeks, and I could feel the exposed tendons at the back of my neck. To make matters worse, my hair was no longer richly blond but a dull shade called mousy brown, the colour of the hair close to my head that hadn't been sun-bleached. I felt as if I'd been turned inside out and was now so ugly I'd have to wear a bag over my head for the rest of my life. The haircut made my teeth seem as huge as a horse's and my neck as long and as scrawny as a chicken's. The pixie cut wasn't making *me* act lighthearted or happy the way it did Elsie. It was making me miserable and ashamed.

"It'll grow out soon enough," Elsie offered. "It's not so bad, really. It's kind of cute."

"Cute?" I wailed. "You call having no hair cute?"

"Don't be so dramatic. Lots of girls have short hair."

"I look like a boy. Like a big, ugly boy. Everyone will laugh at me."

"No, they won't," Elsie said. She sounded absolutely sure.

Ernie was watching *The Three Stooges* when we got home. He laughed when he saw me. "What happened to you? You look like something the cat dragged in. You look like Curly Joe."

"See?" I hollered. "I look like one of the Three Stooges."

Elsie turned on him, the first time in days. "What's the matter with you?" she hissed. "What did you have to say that for?"

He shrugged and went back to the TV. He was watching our all-time favourite Three Stooges episode, "Sing a Song of Six Pants." But I didn't stop to watch, tempted though I was. Instead, I headed to my bedroom so I could slam the door.

"Nyuk, nyuk, nyuk," Curly Joe cackled from the TV set.

ELSIE HAD A MIRROR in her compact case, and so did Doreen. They'd frequently worry over their reflections, anxiously dabbing their noses with powder puffs, carefully applying lipstick as if they were doing a paint-by-numbers picture. It was clear a woman's or a girl's face was only made real by looking in a mirror. If there was no mirror to look at for confirmation, even if you wore makeup, you were faceless.

My brush-and-comb set with the hand mirror was kept on my dresser. I'd never used the hand mirror before. Now I did, checking the back of my head, the sides. Without the ponytail my head felt weightless. The square mirror on my bedroom dresser that only last week had revealed the blur of a girl running by now slowed everything down to a merciless scrutiny. I was like some hopeless princess who would never be the fairest of them all, not in a million fairy tales. I cried, loud and long. Mostly I was outraged that I'd been made to succumb to Rae-Ella against my will.

Naturally I refused to come out of my room when supper was announced.

"Good," Elsie laughed on the other side of the door. "Rip can have your steak."

"I'm not coming out until my hair grows back!"

"Even better! It'll be quiet around here for a change."

Then I heard Elsie and Ernie laughing. Together. Against me.

I crouched by my door, listening. I could hear Ernie's continued huh-huh-ing away. Lately he'd been doing a lot of huh-huhing, not actually laughing out loud, but the kind of vocal smiling a baby does when it has gas. I listened to them eat supper, their chewing sounds, Ernie blowing his nose, Elsie's sudden laugh (I couldn't hear why), and even Rip, the traitor, whining at Ernie's knee for food. "Here boy, have a nice piece of gristle."

Then came dessert – apple pie – when Elsie said, "Cup of tea, dear?" Dear! That cinched it; they'd joined forces against me. This bothered me more than the haircut.

AT SEVEN DOREEN KNOCKED on my door. I hadn't heard her car in the driveway; Elsie must have phoned. "Can I come in?"

"No!" It was exquisite to act so aggrieved.

She came in anyway. I dived beneath a pillow leaving one eye free, pleased she was here. She had an overnight case with her. "Makeup and hair stuff," she explained. Good, kind Doreen. *Repulsive, vile, loathsome* Marion. (I'd looked up "ugly" in the dictionary.)

"Mom told me about your hair." She looked at me closely. "It's not so bad. Makes you look older. Here, let me fix it."

I submitted, making sure to pout, resist a little. She got to work, seating me before my dresser mirror. She backcombed and sprayed, and sprayed some more. My flat limp hair expanded like rising bread dough beneath her fingers. A miracle! I started to soften; maybe I didn't look so bad. I could almost see myself as a Debbie Reynolds look-alike.

"You look quite pretty," Doreen said dubiously when she'd finished. "Really and truly."

I crept out of my bedroom, self-conscious. It was tempting, though, to believe I might now look like the swan instead of the ugly duckling. Ernie looked up from *Davy Crockett* and laughed out loud.

"You look like you've got a balloon stuck on your head," he said.

"Oh, Pop."

Elsie poked her head into the den. "Now your mother will be pleased," she said, like a clairvoyant. "You look so much better. So grown-up."

"I'm thinking of getting the same haircut," Doreen said. "It's really nifty. And no work to look after. Think how much better it will be after swimming. It'll be dry in minutes." She looked at me with a pained expression. "You'll get used to it," she soothed.

"She still looks like she's got a balloon on her head," Ernie repeated, smirking.

"Shut up," Elsie and Doreen said at the same time.

TWENTY-SIX

Ernie and Elsie

On day two before Nancy's visit, Elsie won the cam-
paign to recapture Ernie's heart. He came home from work as usual
but left right away, saying, "I've got to see a man about a dog."

"Dog? Are we getting another dog?"

"Just an expression," Elsie said, glancing up from the sewing machine
where she was working on the skirt and blouse I was to wear for N-Day.
I thought Ernie was going to see Mrs. Johns. But Elsie was calm.

An hour later he returned home carrying a budgie in a cage.

"You got it!" Elsie smiled, giving him a peck on the cheek.

The idea of the budgie had started with Rae-Ella, of course, who had got one for her shop, a squawky blue thing named Oscar. All the customers made a fuss over it, and Elsie had been yakking nonstop about wanting a budgie ever since. And now Ernie had bought her one as a surprise.

The cage was bell shaped and made of metal. The budgie came with a bag of toys. "Look!" Elsie showed me, happily unwrapping a small box. "A little bell for his cage."

Ernie bent over the cage. "Who's a pretty boy, then?" he said gently. "Who's a pretty thing?" He made kissing sounds. The bird kept cocking its head as if it was trying to catch the words.

"What's its name?" I asked, peering at the tiny thing. It had a yellow breast and turquoise feathers and was hopping along a thin pole that stretched across the cage.

"Chee-Chee," Ernie said.

"Chee-Chee?"

"Chee-Chee," Ernie repeated. "It's a name from South America. That's where budgies come from."

Elsie tinkled the unwrapped bell. "Cute, isn't it?"

They bent over the cage cooing at the bird, Elsie's stiff bouffant hair grazing Ernie's shiny dome.

Later Ernie and I were watching *Bonanza*. We could hear Elsie grunting away in her room. "Ernie," she called. "Give me a hand?" We both went. She was pulling the sewing bench away from his side of the bed.

"Here, let me do that," he said, overly sweet I thought, and shoved it against the wall. Elsie took down the ironing board. There was a lot of bumping into each other on purpose. And giggles. Disgusted, I went back to the TV.

That night, after I'd gone to sleep, he moved back into her room.

I didn't know exactly how Elsie had dispatched the rival Mrs. Johns – other than with good meals – but I overheard her on the phone the next morning talking long-distance to Shirley in California. She was standing with the receiver under her chin, holding an ashtray with one hand and tapping a cigarette into it with the other.

"Well," she was saying, "first Maudie and me had a good look at the woman. At Evelyn's Café. That's right. All the way downtown. Last Tuesday. No, Doreen wanted to come, but we thought three was too many. So it was just Maudie and me. We went into the coffee shop and had a cup of tea at the counter while Mrs. Johns was at work. What did she look like? Plain. Ordinary. Nothing to write home about. Tired-looking with thin, dark hair. Kind of pathetic, really, in her white uniform. Having to work like that. Leaving her son at home. What? Oh, no, we never let on. She didn't know who we were. We drank our tea and tried not to look obvious watching her. She didn't do much. Just cleaned the counter and fiddled with the milkshake machine. There was only one other person in the place. An old man in a booth."

Elsie listened for a moment.

"It was easy," she said, and laughed. "After I found out about Ernie and her, I just beefed up my attentions to him. What with the food and the extra desserts he never knew what hit him. Butter wouldn't melt in his mouth now. It's like night and day. Hah! Mildred can eat her tarts and cookies all by herself. She can have tea with her bloody dog."

TWENTY-SEVEN

Marion and Nancy

The dictionary. Originally it had been Billy's, a worn Concise Oxford that he kept in his grip to do crossword puzzles on the weekends he visited. I'd borrowed it so many times he'd finally given it to me the year before and bought himself another. When the dictionary was fully mine, I scratched out Billy's name on the inside cover – *W.D. Gibson* – and beneath it, copying Billy, wrote my own name: *M.A. Gibson.* It was a revelation, seeing my name like that. I liked the strength that the initials imparted, as solid as a pair of Greek columns. I was astonished at the way initials could cleave a life. Billy's: owner of a broken heart, *and* W.D., captain of ships. Likewise Marion: *Wiss Warion Gibson,* child of an errant mother, *and* M.A., wielder of words.

It was the Third Edition Oxford, with pages as thin as tissue paper and a cracked spine held together with thick electrical tape from Ernie's shop. 1,566 pages, including appendices. Two inches thick. The compressed pages when the book was shut were so worn with thumbprints and grime that they were yellowy-beige in colour and felt like velvet. No one seemed to understand what the book meant to me, that it was more than a listing of words. It was a secret trove, a treasure chest: the source, I believed, of a special power, one that enabled me to dumbfound and amaze, most frequently myself. The book was so important it never left my room.

School-issue dictionaries were meager things by comparison, laughable, with easily torn paper covers, large child-friendly print, and a scant two hundred pages. Like an infant, you were made to print your name on the cover using only one initial, the last: Marion G.

My Oxford dictionary, substantial and unique, sat on the end of my dresser, a bestseller among the small collection of books I kept there. Mostly my reading of it was random, often idle. Sometimes it was deliberate. I'd hear a word used at school, something a teacher had called a kid – "nitwit." I'd look it up first thing after school. Same for "penis," after Mr. Wilson, my science teacher, casually mentioned the word during his talk on mammals; I knew what it meant but not fully. This led to the thrilling realization that the dictionary contained other words, *associated words,* like clues in a game of Capture the Flag – *copulate, orifice, reproduction, sex, vagina.* And the prize was always more words, stepping stones to greater and greater marvels. Reading the dictionary, I was Marion Alice in Wonderland, a girl by turns puzzled, mystified, elated, and engaged. Instead of wandering about at the bottom of a black hole, I was scurrying along with my nose close to the pages of this rarest of books.

Although Elsie complained that I used dictionary words to confound her, I don't think she fully realized that reading it was also the source of that other colossal fault, having a mind of my own. I'd hurl words at her like fireballs and picture her melting before me like the Wicked Witch in *The Wizard of Oz*. She'd hurl back her own accusations, dismissing my assaults as "showing off" or "acting uppity." To her a dictionary was something boring beyond belief, and so not a real threat; anyone who read one for pleasure was an egghead, though she never called me that. But her disdain for books in general contributed magnificently to their appeal.

On the morning of Nancy's arrival I was in my room. My clothes lay across the bed: new blouse, new skirt, clean underwear, socks. My new shoes, the white ones, so-called grown-up shoes because they didn't have straps, were placed on the floor beneath the skirt. It looked as if an invisible girl lay on her back across my bed, leaving only her deflated clothes as proof of her existence.

I was supposed to be getting ready for the trip to the airport.

Maybe it was because of my shorn hair and the boils and my belief that the mirror told the truth: I was ugly now beyond all hope, a cretin, an object of ridicule. Maybe it was because Nancy's visit had come to resemble a false Christmas, with the excitement and the overwrought preparations. Maybe it was because I'd been largely ignored during this time. Other than the uproar over my haircut, everyone was too busy to notice me scowling from the sidelines.

But on impulse I reached for the dictionary. Standing there in my shorts and bare feet I looked up the word "mother." I was surprised I'd never done this before. I was surprised I felt nervous doing so now. *MOTHER transitive verb* to give birth to; protect as a mother; acknowledge or profess oneself the mother of a child.

Score: one out of three.

It was the dictionary that decided me.

I put my bathing suit on beneath my shorts and slipped out, leaving the new clothes on the bed. Elsie and Ernie were in the kitchen; I crept along the other side of the house so as not to be seen. Then I ran. Aggrieved. Sullen. Yet thrilled, too.

There was still dew on the grass along the pathway down to the beach; my feet and legs were wet when I got to the bottom. The tide was fairly high, the sky hazy, the morning hot. I ran along the foreshore, through patches of sand and stones, dodged driftwood and clamshells. Rip was beside me. Below Smith's store I sat down, resting against a log, and faced the water. This is where I stayed. Few people were about. For a long while I saw only an old woman walking a terrier.

I sat there, and I wasn't going to move. It was because everything had gone along like a fast-flowing river and there were things I could not stop. Because I hadn't heard anyone say "no" to Nancy: "No, you can't come. No, we're too busy. We're going on holiday. We don't want you here." It was because everyone dumbly fell into line with whatever Nancy felt like doing: dropping a daughter, picking up a daughter, like a pointless game of jacks. Because no one had told her, "Marion's ours, not yours. She doesn't belong to you anymore."

I don't know why I believed my defiance would make a difference. But I did believe that. So I sat on the beach, refusing the meeting. Saying "no" to Nancy myself, firm in my resolve that I didn't want her, did not belong to her, wanted nothing of her.

IT DIDN'T TAKE ELSIE long to have a story to tell about Nancy's visit. Later that summer I listened at the patio door while, outside over tea, Elsie told Mrs. Holt what had happened. By then everyone in the family, including me, was content with her version.

> That Nancy thought she was the bloody Queen. I should have known better than to get swept up in things, planning everything the way I did. I should have known from that time when Marion was six years old. We got a call then, too, saying Nancy was coming back. Billy had sent her money for the boat trip. After I found out what he'd done, I said to him, "She'll only spend it on herself. Mark my words." But Billy paid no notice to me. Abrupt he was. "It's all arranged," he said. So I shut my mouth. If he wanted to believe Nancy was coming back, that was his business. But I was right; she never turned up.

This visit was just the same. Like an old song. I don't know what led us to believe it would be different. We were like a bunch of fools all over again. We got everything ready. We cooked and cleaned. We cancelled our trip to Grand Coulee Dam. Everything was turned upside down because of Nancy. The things I had to put up with during those weeks leading to the visit. Marion was impossible, as you can imagine, and so wound up – the tantrums, the yelling. She banged her bedroom door so many times she finally broke the hinges. Ernie had to take off the door to fix it.

On July 14, Nancy was supposed to be on the eleven o'clock plane. She was supposed to fly to Vancouver from the boat in Los Angeles and then fly to the Island. After breakfast Marion disappeared. At nine thirty I noticed she was gone. "Where's Marion?" I said to Ernie. He was outside washing the car, getting it ready to pick up Her Ladyship. He said he hadn't seen her.

Everything was ready for the visit. The food, the house, Maudie's house. I'd made Marion a new cotton skirt and blouse for the occasion. The skirt was solid turquoise, the blouse, a pretty turquoise print with puff sleeves. I'd worked late the night before so they'd be ready in time. I found the clothes still on the bed when I looked in her room. Then I noticed Rip was gone, too. "Ernie," I called, "Marion's gone." We were supposed to leave for the airport at ten fifteen and here it was nine thirty.

"She's probably on the beach," he said. So we went to look for her. I was all dressed, ready to go, and had to climb down the bank in my stockings and high heels, Ernie behind me helping me over the rougher bits. You probably saw me from your kitchen window and wondered what was going on. When we reached the sand he spotted the dog way down the beach by Smith's store. I couldn't go any farther in my clothes but Ernie could. It was hot out, and I sat on a log and watched Ernie hurry along the beach. He was gone a long time, then finally came back with the dog.

"She won't come," he said. "Says we can't make her." It was ten by now. We had to leave for the airport.

"Well, she can bloody well stay home," I said. I was so mad at her. She was so flighty and unpredictable. But I had no idea she'd do this, be so defiant. She liked the outfit I'd made her, she even said so. I thought she wanted to wear it. Driving to the airport I said to Ernie, "What was Marion doing down there?" "Nothing much," he said. "Just sitting in the sand and playing with her feet." "Playing with her feet?" I said. I mean, really.

Ernie said she was covering up her feet with sand and staring out at the water. He said she didn't seem upset, just that she'd made up her mind.

"Well, it's the bloody end!" I said. I mean there's no controlling her, she does what she likes. And Billy does bugger all about it. Nothing. He always sides with Marion against me. After all I've done for her. After all I've done for him!

Ernie warned me years ago when we first took Marion, as you know. He said I shouldn't get so involved. That she wasn't my daughter, she belonged to someone else. He said it would only break my heart, that I'd only get hurt. But that day driving to the airport I wasn't hurt, only mad.

The plane was late. We sat on those hard wooden benches in the waiting room for over an hour before the plane finally came in. Then we looked out the window expecting to see Nancy in the group of people heading towards the waiting room. She'll be the one all dolled up, I was thinking, dressed to the nines, putting the rest of us to shame. It was a small plane and I counted every person that came off it. I counted to nineteen. And that was it. We asked someone in charge where Mrs. Gibson was. He looked at the list and said, "There's no Mrs. Gibson here. But there's a Nancy Whitehouse who didn't get on the plane."

"That's her," I said. "Whitehouse was her maiden name." For some reason this made me mad, too. That she'd be using her maiden name and not Gibson, not Marion and Billy's name.

We didn't know what to do then.

Ernie said we might as well go home and phone Billy. Try and find out what had happened. Maybe Nancy had missed the plane and would come later. Maybe it wasn't her fault. We asked when the next plane from Vancouver came in and were told there was only one, at seven that night.

So we went home. Marion still wasn't there. But I noticed she'd been in the kitchen. She'd been in the fridge and left the milk bottle on the counter. Right away I tried phoning Billy in Vancouver but couldn't reach him and I didn't know where he was. I phoned Maudie then because the supper for Nancy would be ruined. I phoned Doreen, too, and she started crying when I told her Marion had run off. She said she'd come out.

We sat by the phone all afternoon. Doreen came and left Lyn with me and went down the beach after Marion. When she came back an hour later Marion wasn't with her, but she said the pair of them had been swimming. "You've been swimming," I said, "when I'm here worrying myself sick!"

She told me Marion would come home for supper but that she wasn't going to the airport for the second trip either, nothing could make her.

"I'm going to throttle her when I see her," I said. "After what she's put us through." I meant it, too.

At four thirty Billy phoned. Said he'd got a telegram from Nancy. "She's not coming," he said. I asked him why not, but he wasn't saying much. He never liked to talk about Nancy. All he would say was, "It didn't work out, what with the flights." So it was plain that Nancy wasn't coming. And that was that.

Right away Doreen went back down the beach and got Marion. When they traipsed in the house they were arm in arm, both of them grinning, acting like nothing in the world was wrong.

"You can wipe those bloody smiles off your faces," I told them. "If I ever live through another day like this one I don't know what I'll do. Nobody ever thinks about what I feel, what I have to put up with."

I couldn't help it. I broke down. Just thinking of all the baking and cleaning I'd done, not to mention sewing that outfit for Marion. And the way our trip was cancelled because of Nancy, the trip everyone was looking forward to, that was the most upsetting thing.

I was sitting in the den crying my bloody eyes out when Ernie said, "We can still go." I looked at him. I was so shocked. "We can leave the day after tomorrow," he said. "Phone Billy. He can meet us on the other side."

So that's what we did. Doreen and Bob and Lyn came out to the Bay to look after the house and Rip, and they brought Grandma and looked after her as well. We had our trip to Grand Coulee Dam after all.

It was a pretty good trip. For the first time in living memory Marion was perfect. Behaved herself the whole time, no running off in a snit. The only thing that went wrong was when she threw up in Astoria, Oregon, on the sidewalk outside a place that sold taffy. Maudie bought a bottle of Castoria for her and then Billy joked for the rest of the trip about Marion having Castoria in Astoria.

But we put Nancy behind us. We enjoyed ourselves. Although I'd have to admit, Grand Coulee Dam wasn't all it's cracked up to be. It was miserable out the day we visited. We were with a bunch of people and a tour guide standing on top of the dam in the rain looking down at a lot of brown water. What makes this the Eighth Wonder of the World, I said to myself? It was like watching water come out of a drainpipe. So if you're going to the States, I wouldn't recommend Grand Coulee Dam. A waste of time. Go instead to the J.C. Penney store in Portland, Oregon. That's where Maudie and me bought sheets and towels. The prices were so cheap, half of what you'd pay in Canada. Everything's cheap in the States. Chocolate bars, tinned fruit. And you get free refills of coffee in the restaurants. Did you know that? As many cups as you like. So all in all, the trip gave us nothing to complain about. The scenery was interesting and the motels were clean.

I nodded with satisfaction as Elsie finished talking. This had become my favourite story of hers. I called it "Her Bloody Ladyship."

1964

TWENTY-EIGHT

Marion

A coiffed girl wearing a pink-satin gown and matching high-heeled shoes sits in Elsie and Ernie's living room having her picture taken. It's 1964. She's seventeen and she's going to the ball (her boyfriend's high school dance). It's Cinderella! And there's the hovering fairy godmother (Billy) and the kindly coachman (Ernie) and the loyal songbird making the stunning gown with thread held aloft in her teeth (Elsie in the Disney version). The ugly stepmother (Nancy) is never talked about, never even thought of.

"Congratulations!" Billy had exclaimed with greater and louder frequency throughout these years to 1964. What looked to be a ship negotiating a rough voyage – boils, shorn hair, the spectre of Nancy's return – managed to find the glassy calm of a safe harbour. The metamorphosis, he believed, had been a success. Everything was fine now, thank you; everything was shipshape. We got through the worst of the teenage years. Didn't we? We did. Although none of us saw what was on the horizon like a cowboy rescue – the *real* sixties, eighteen months away.

In the photo I'm wearing long white gloves and holding a gardenia wrist corsage. The living room at Cordova Bay was used only at Christmas or for special occasions. It was a room as neat, though not as classy, as a display room at Standard Furniture, the best furniture store in Victoria: couch and chair covered in turquoise brocade; floral print drapes; coffee and end tables made by Ernie out of tiles with stained wood trim and thin, splayed legs; turquoise wall-to-wall carpet; the never-used fireplace; the best ornaments on show – a pair of black panthers, the cocker spaniel dog. Billy took the picture.

By now my reading for pleasure – Mark Twain! – was a thing of the past, my well-loved dictionary shoved to the back of my bedroom closet. I looked only at schoolbooks, and only because I had to.

I never went to the beach, either, unless it was for sunbathing with my girlfriends, our transistor radios blasting Motown hits from KJR in Seattle. Nor was I seen splashing about in the water, for fear of dinting the stiff blond helmet that was my hair. I was held together with hairspray and CoverGirl foundation. Reined in with girdles, garter belts, and an overwhelming terror of getting knocked up, of being called a slut. I was a cosseted, even demure, female, yet frequently haughty, frequently filled with the heat of restrained excitement. Forget childhood dreams of writing and starring in Broadway musicals or even of owning a kennel. The only thing I wanted now was to be popular. The most popular. The queen.

I found myself at the centre of the in-group at school, a fearsome knot of six – Paulette, Sherry, Dana, Lynne with an *E*, plain Lynn, and me – who ruled our junior and senior classes: all of us in the "smart class"; all of us "best-looking" and on the students' council, running the school paper. Doris had skipped a grade and moved in her own circle now.

Bob no longer called me Hi Sexy! Now it was Pus Lips, after the thick white lipstick I wore.

"Oh, Bob, don't be such a drip." I couldn't be brought down.

"Pus lips! Pus lips!"

"Oh, Bob. Dry up."

There were boys, of course, herds of them. Sullenly handsome boys seen slouching in their cars at the White Spot drive-in in Victoria on Friday and Saturday nights. And excessive yearning for a steady boyfriend and the right to wear a signet ring on a chain around my neck – Larry's ring, Pat's ring. There were movies, parties, more dances. There was necking in cars at the top of Mount Doug or Mount Tolmie or at Island View Beach or even in my driveway, with boys named Phil, Roger, Roddy, Walter, Pat. Careful to go only so far. Yet hot with the struggle, car windows steaming from hours of kissing, feeling, panting.

At sixteen I learned to drink and drive, though not together. First came driving lessons with Ernie in his pickup, me wearing high heels and nylons just like Elsie did to conquer gearshift and clutch. Sounding like her, too, with my girlfriends: "Imagine! Me! Driving my uncle's dirty old truck." No one could.

Learning to drink was harder; I never did succeed. There were determined attempts, though, and weekend nights of lemon gin, vodka and orange, rye and ginger ale. It was no use. After three drinks I'd throw up. Every time. It was the same with cigarettes; I'd get dizzy. I was beginning to suspect a Christian Science plot engineered by Mrs. Holt. My girlfriends would console me. "You look like someone who *should* smoke," they'd say pityingly, blowing perfect smoke rings, sharing drags.

I learned a few other things, too. That whatever will be, will be (the Doris Day song). That blond streaks in your hair will get rid of the "mousy look" (the dashing Mr. Gerard, Victoria hairdresser). That you should never eat wild mushrooms because they'll kill you (grade eleven science teacher). That it's not *really* important if you don't keep the inside of your fridge spotlessly clean (Maudie). That "men only want one thing and if you don't give it to them, they get mad" and also that if you're not careful, men will make you their slave (Elsie). That "nice" girls don't smoke, drink, or go all the way (Mrs. Holt) and that if you get knocked up, "your life will be over" (grade eleven guidance teacher, Miss Horel). That you should be kind and never break up with a boy before he has a final exam, but breaking up before *other* exams is okay (Mrs. Holt). That only sluts and ignorant people wear white before the May 24 weekend (Doreen). That there's no rule that says you must love your children (Nancy), but on the other hand, they're a mixed blessing, because something is always going the matter with them (Mrs. Holt). That it's all family, nothing else is worth the effort (Elsie). That everything was better in England (Maudie). That everything is better now (Elsie). That you should buy a new car every couple of years (Billy).

TWENTY-NINE

Marion

Billy bought a new car in the spring of 1964, a Pontiac Parisienne. A two-door hardtop convertible. The colour: pink on the bottom, white on top. I thought I'd died and gone to heaven. It dwarfed the house; it was as long as a limousine. The chrome on the fenders winked like silver fillings in a perpetually grinning mouth. The inside of the car was white leather, the carpets pink. The colour of the car matched my pink princess telephone. A few times I was allowed to take the car to school. Or fill it with Paulette, Sherry, Dana, Lynne, and Lynn on weekend nights, driving along Pat Bay Highway to the White Spot or the A&W for cheeseburgers and Cokes. Boys in lowered hot rods cruised by and stared. Once to the Tillicum Drive-In for the double feature – movie speakers tilting out from the windows, paper baskets filled with ketchup-smothered fries on our laps.

Elsie took the car to her new part-time job at Butchart Gardens, where she worked in the gift shop. She needed to sit on two cushions to drive it. It had power steering; Billy said it could "turn on a dime." Ernie drove it, but never in his work clothes; Elsie made him dress up. She dressed up to drive it, too. Everyone dressed up. The car was like an astonishingly beautiful guest that we were showing around. It was something we had to live up to; it set us apart. The car meant there was no denying it: we had come up in the world. We were suddenly, unbelievably, anointed with prestige and wealth.

We'd go for Sunday afternoon drives when Billy was over. Everyone came: Maudie, Elsie, Ernie, Doreen, Bob, Lyn (now five) on someone's lap, and once even Kenny, laughing his head off over the paint job. Five of us could sit comfortably in the back; three, sometimes four (always the men), in the front. Billy was at the wheel for these drives, wearing a jaunty white panama hat, his elbow hooked casually over the window-sill. We were so proud of what he'd accomplished – this fabulous car! No one we knew owned anything like it. It was way better than the cars parked by the side of the road at Beacon Hill Park, or the ones we whizzed by on the highway, where we'd be flying along some bright afternoon heading nowhere in particular. "Drive on, chauffeur," Elsie would call in a la-de-da voice, dangling her wrist. "Take us for a spin." Once Bob turned around with an amazed look on his face. We were driving along licking double-headed ice cream cones – chocolate, maple walnut, Neopolitan. "I wonder what the poor people are doing!" he said. Maudie cried out, "Cripes!" and laughed. Everyone laughed. At the very idea.

Grandma had died a week before her eighty-ninth birthday. Maudie woke one morning to find her dead in bed beside her. "She looked like she was smiling in her sleep," Maudie told us, "and she was still warm."

Elsie and Ernie had the funeral tea. Everyone sat on the patio facing the traffic and reminisced about Grandma and the bottles of beer she'd hurled down the sink, how her hat had been stapled to the carport roof, how she was a character, a card. They laughed and said "Eh?" over and over. Elsie baked a ham and a cherry pie. Maudie still supplied the potato salad.

Grandma took up residence in Ross Bay Cemetery beside the others, Grandpa and Frank, achieving a new kind of importance as the latest subject of the cemetery visits. They'd buried her with her hearing aid still in and wearing her black hat and her best black-silk dress, the one covered with tiny grey flowers. They put a pack of cards in the coffin.

ERNIE HAD REMAINED IN the double bed with Elsie. By now their bickering had resumed, though they were quieter about it; it never erupted into the grim battles of previous years. The two of them took up square dancing. Every Wednesday night they went to the Women's Institute on Quadra Street in Victoria and square danced with a group called the Belles and Beaux. Elsie sewed special square-dance dresses for herself, full-skirted ones in yellow, turquoise, and red with contrasting rickrack stitched around the neck and sleeves and hems. She made Ernie matching shirts with the same rickrack trim and a small coordinating towel with a loop to go through his belt, something that all the men square dancers used so their hands wouldn't be sweaty during the allemande lefts and the do-si-dos.

I quit dancing in the winter of 1964 because it was interfering with my social life. And I was getting nowhere with Miss Blythe, who thought that dancing was more important than dating and never did give me an important solo part. I never managed to become her favourite pupil, either, probably because of the imitations I did of her. She was a shrill woman who often harangued us and was not above humiliating one girl in front of another. She walked into the dressing room once when I was entertaining a group of students, screeching at them in a maniacal German accent, "You vill do two thousand demi-pliés in the next half-hour, and there is no escape ..."

I'd been going to three practices a week and, as Doreen and Shirley had done, performed in floor shows on the weekends – at the Boiler-makers Hall, at William Head Prison for the Dale Carnegie support group, at weddings and fundraisers. There were eight of us in the troupe and we were called the Miss Blythe Dancers, supposedly in evocation of the showgirl dancers – the June Taylor Dancers – seen on *The Ed Sullivan Show*. We did the cancan, the hula, a few tap numbers, and, during the Charleston, a kind of striptease where we wiggled out of our dresses and flung them to the floor, revealing ourselves in black-satin suits with a lot of leg and cleavage showing. I overheard one of the inmates at the prison sum up our performance as jailbait, though none of us thought we were anything other than wholesome, innocent, Judy Garland look-alikes putting on a show for the troops. Our pay for these shows was five dollars a night, Miss Blythe keeping sixty of the hundred-dollar fee for herself.

The solo part I was finally given for my last recital was a minor one as the Wicked Witch in *The Wizard of Oz*, a part I found humiliating. I longed, of course, to be Dorothy or Glinda, the Good Witch, but those parts went to compliant girls like Denise and Beverley, who had flowing waist-length hair; my metal-stiff beehive was hardly the hair of lead dancers. Being the Wicked Witch meant wearing a shapeless long black dress, a pointed witch's hat, and green face paint. There was much twirling about and screeching. Miss Blythe must have enjoyed the spectacle, though Elsie was grim. There was the uninteresting dress to sew, the difficult hat to make out of cardboard and black paint, the embarrassing lack of glamour associated with the part.

I was seventeen and Elsie still claimed that I was spoiled and willful, that you couldn't tell me "a single bloody thing." We were still engaged in our love-hate pas de deux; that much hadn't changed, though we had softened towards each other by now. There were fewer histrionics, more heated negotiations. She said I wore too much makeup, dressed too glamorously for school, dated too many boys, even though she con-tinued to sew for me the skirts, dresses, and coats that were the envy of my girlfriends. She had inflexible rules that I complained about bitterly but nevertheless followed. If I didn't it meant I couldn't drive the Parisienne.

[THIRTY]

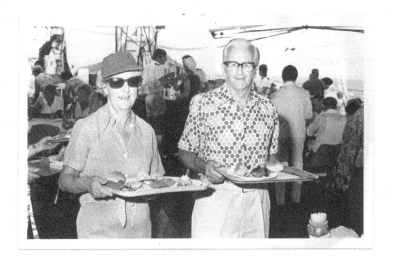

Nancy and Stan

In September of 1964, Nancy re-entered the picture.
It was almost "Who's Nancy?" by then. She didn't seem to matter much anymore; she was seldom mentioned. After the failed visit four years earlier, the stories about her petered out. Everyone – especially me – lost interest.

I took the phone call from Billy. "She's coming in on the *Canberra*," he shouted down the line (he always shouted when he was calling long distance). "She'll be in Vancouver in a week's time." He said I could take the Parisienne over to Vancouver to meet her and have his bachelor apartment to myself. He'd stay at the Y.

"Here we go again," Elsie said when I told her. "Do you want me to go with you?" she asked, adding, "I wouldn't bother if I were you. What's the point?"

But I said I wanted to go by myself.

Since Nancy's last no-show, there'd been a couple of letters and cards from her telling me about her six Pekingese dogs, her trips on cruise ships, her new husband, Stanley. Always written with that strange handwriting, the *M*'s and *W*'s reversed. But I'd long given up studying her writing for hidden meaning as if it were hieroglyphics. The only gift I received from her during this time was a gold lamé evening bag that I used with my semiformal dresses; it arrived out of the blue in the middle of winter.

This time Nancy came. I was standing on the Vancouver dock beside Billy when the ship arrived; the only other people around were dockworkers. Billy had a megaphone in his hand and was guiding the *Canberra*, as huge as a high-rise, into the berth. "Another half-inch, John," he called up to the first mate, joking even then.

I had on a white-wool suit that Elsie had made and black high heels, and I felt sophisticated and strong. My hair was swept into a beehive with a fake braid attached above the bangs, and I was wearing the pearl drop earrings Billy had given me for my birthday. I felt expensive. One of the main things I knew about Nancy was that she "wore clothes well," and I believed I could match her. It helped that the Parisienne was parked in the VIP section at the end of the dock, looking like an advertisement in a glossy magazine.

Crowds of people hung over the railings on several levels of the ship as it edged into the berth. Then I heard a woman's high-pitched voice – "Yoo-hoo, Marion!" – and looked up to see, high above me, a tiny figure waving a white handkerchief.

When she came down the gangway she was with her new husband, Stanley. My first reaction was one of shock because she was so tiny and so much older than I'd imagined. To my eyes she seemed almost shrivelled, though she was dressed well, of course, in a turquoise-silk suit and mink stole. Stanley was even older, white-haired with waxy-looking skin. Nancy and I embraced, stiffly. "Oh, you're so much taller than me!" she said. I thought she sounded annoyed. I turned around to look for Billy, but he'd vanished.

It was late afternoon. The ship would be berthed until the following morning. I ushered them to the Parisienne. Nancy got into the passenger seat, Stanley into the back, and I drove them to dinner, through Vancouver traffic to a seafood restaurant. Billy had given me money for the meal.

Our conversation during dinner was halting, strained. Nancy asked a few perfunctory questions about school and my future plans. To my brief answers, she said, "Yayess," with that distinctive Australian accent. I kept watching her, trying to find a physical connection. I thought we looked nothing alike. She was tiny, brown-eyed. I was tall by comparison, and my eyes were green. She wore bright-orange lipstick that bent the corners of her mouth into a downward arch, like a sad clown's; her hair was dark with a magenta rinse, but thin, brittle, cut short and curled like an old woman's. There were several diamond rings on her fingers; her fingernails were painted the Chinese red I remembered from years ago. She picked at her salmon steak. After she spoke she'd make a little humming sound; it was as if she were singing to herself, perhaps as a way to bridge the awkward silences. I flailed around for things to talk about. I was curious about Australia because of being born there and asked about the Aboriginal Australians.

"I don't have much interest in the them," Nancy said dismissively. "They're just there. Some of their paintings are all right. In the caves. They claim they're two thousand years old. But you can't be sure. They could have done them last week for all we know."

Stanley, meanwhile, said nothing. He had something the matter with him and could eat only salad. But I knew he was wealthy; in her infrequent letters Nancy had mentioned that he owned hotels.

I wondered what Nancy was thinking of me. I was hoping she'd find me exquisite but beyond her grasp. That she'd be envious, jealous of the car, of my youth and my pearl earrings, of my father who could single-handedly guide a massive cruise ship into a narrow berth. I was hoping she'd regret missing her daughter's life, not that I was prepared to give it back to her.

But she gave no indication of what she thought or felt; she hardly looked at me.

I drove them back to the ship.

As arranged I stayed the night in Billy's apartment. It was on the ground floor of a large, old manor house and could be reached through a wood-panelled entry. The large, high-ceilinged room had Billy's single bed in one corner, a couple of easy chairs, an alcove for a kitchen, a walk-in closet, and a small bathroom. There was no TV, only a radio.

The phone was ringing as I unlocked the door. It was Billy. "How'd you make out?"

"All right."

"How'd the car behave?"

"Okay."

"Right, then. You'd better be getting to bed. It's late." He gave me the number at the Y.

I said good night and, for the first time in years, called him Daddy.

I pulled the curtains, rechecked that the door was locked, and got into bed. There was now only the soapy smell of Billy's wool blankets, the moving shadows of trees through the curtain, the phone on the bedside table.

The next morning I picked up Nancy and Stan and took them for breakfast at a nearby restaurant. Nancy seemed bored. I was astonished to see Stanley cutting the crusts off her toast and fawning over her as if she were helpless, an invalid. "Are you warm enough, darling?" "Tea hot enough, darling?" It was raining heavily. Nancy seemed affronted by the damp and the cold, an unpleasant memory, perhaps, of those trapped, long-ago months in Vancouver. She complained that her mink stole was getting wet.

After breakfast we returned to the ship. Nancy took me into their stateroom, which was large and above deck, and then into a small walk-in closet. There she showed me her clothes, one beaded gown after another. And her jewellery – an emerald earring-and-necklace set, strands of pearls, a ruby brooch. She showed me her shoes: white-satin high-heeled slippers trimmed in white marabou, evening shoes in brocade with glass beads glued onto the toes. We didn't speak, really; it was just Nancy flipping through the clothes and displaying her jewels. As an afterthought she pulled a silk scarf from a drawer filled with silk scarves and gave it to me. It was blue with a brown design of palm trees spread across it. "It'll match your eyes," she said distractedly, though whether she thought my eyes were blue or brown I didn't know.

After that we moved outside to sit on the deck. The ship was leaving in an hour's time, and visitors had to disembark in thirty minutes. Next stop was Hawai'i. But within ten minutes I got up to leave because Nancy had fallen asleep. Her head had slumped to one side and she was snoring lightly. I said goodbye to Stan, who looked up and gave me a small smile; he was gently arranging a blanket over Nancy's knees.

I thought perhaps Nancy was ill and dying, but this turned out not to be the case. She lived, and rather well in fact, for another twenty-five years. Several months after she returned to Australia she wrote to say how much she'd enjoyed our visit and sent me a picture of her and Stan on board the *Canberra*. She also said – and I thought this was the *real* reason for the letter – that Stan had bought her a new car, a pink Pontiac Parisienne just like Billy's; it had been ordered specially from Canada and shipped to Australia. Years later I found out that she had written to Billy after this visit to ask him to take her back; the car must have led her to believe he was richer than Stan was. Billy said he ignored the letter.

WHEN I GOT HOME from Vancouver, Elsie was waiting for me in the den. It was early afternoon, and she was on the couch with some hand sewing. "How did it go?" she asked, cheerful.

"Fine," I said, and hurried to my bedroom, shutting the door. Shutting her out. But after a few minutes I joined her. I felt bad that my evasion might have hurt her; the story of Nancy, after all, was her story as much as mine. I sat beside her on the couch.

"All she wanted to talk about was her clothes," I told her. "And show me her dresses and jewellery. It was like visiting a stranger. A boring stranger. A boring stranger who's selfish. I don't care if I ever see her again."

Elsie nodded. "I've always said the only person Nancy's ever loved is herself. You would have had a tough time living with your mother."

We left it at that. Because for a long while I'd known what was true. That I'd been lucky to escape Nancy. That I'd done the right thing to keep her at arm's length, pushed away. That her replacement was so much better.

We sat there on the couch. Elsie was sewing buttons on a blouse for Doreen. She said, "You didn't clean out your closet like you were supposed to. It's a pigsty."

"What? I was busy. Remember? I was in Vancouver."

"That's no excuse. You had all week. And don't go thinking you're so smart just because Billy let you take the car ..."

"Nag, nag," I said.

She looked at me. "You sound like Ernie." I laughed. So did she.

ENCORE

COMPANION STORIES

[TRAVELLING GARBAGE]

Ernie, Elsie, Marion, Billy

It was driving along Route 99 in Oregon state during the summer of 1961 that we first saw a giant cartoon bug painted on a billboard. Alongside the picture were the words *Don't Be a Litterbug! Pick Up Your Garbage!*

We laughed when we saw the sign. "Would you look at *that*?"

We were on vacation and that sign was another thing to roar past on the way to the next motel, the one with the adjoining Frontier restaurant specializing in steaks the size of saddles.

The litterbug had a black eye patch, green wings, a black-and-yellow striped body like a bee, and smoked a cigarette. There was a mound of garbage at the litterbug's feet.

A bug was telling us to clean up our garbage. We laughed our heads off; the idea was absurd: there was no family cleaner than ours.

Ernie, my uncle, continually stated the obvious. "What are we, bums?" he'd snort, incredulous, if he found empty pop bottles or gum wrappers inside the car. Riding around in a car filled with garbage was a disgusting thing to do, he said, like riding in the back of a garbage truck and being covered with stinking muck. That's what he called it – stinking muck.

If I was remiss and left a potato-chip bag on the car seat, Ernie would notice right away. Even while driving. Elsie said he had eyes in the back of his head. "You can't get away with nothing with Ernie. So do as you're told and throw that bag out the bloody window."

Unlike the litterbug, there was no mound of garbage at Ernie's feet.

Ernie's vigilance was helped along by the fact that he was the janitor at the Victoria Public Library. He seemed always on duty, prowling the house and yard, keys dangling from the ring attached to his belt. If things weren't spic and span, watch out! "Germs," he'd say ominously, "hide *everywhere*."

Elsie was the same. You'd have thought my aunt and uncle's zealousness would have translated to the outside world. It didn't. The outside world was called Out There and, aside from sunsets and days at the beach, it was a boring place, useful mainly for driving over – and dumping your garbage.

Billy thought the same way: everything had to be "squared away." He said he'd learned this important thing at sea. He also said, "When you live in a stinking mess you can't see what's what." He told me to remember this; it was one of Life's Truths.

But it was Ernie who was our standard bearer as far as travelling garbage went. He made a big production of tossing his cigarette package out the car window. The package went as soon as the last cigarette was hanging off his lip. But first he'd extract the silver foil the cigarettes were wrapped in, folding the two pieces carefully and then putting them into his wallet next to the thick wad of dollar bills. He did this while driving, lifting his bum off the seat in a delicate maneuver to get at the wallet, and then lifting it again to return it there.

Why Ernie saved cigarette foil was a mystery. "Wouldn't you like to know?" he'd smirk, giving me the idea that janitors were people with secret lives. Because I didn't know *exactly* what that secret life might be, I made one up. It happened, I decided, after supper each night when, cranky as usual, he'd lock himself in his workshop off the carport. Inside, I imagined him sitting on the stool beside his prized possession, a huge new table saw, and "working away at his hobby" – fashioning tiny airplanes out of cigarette foil. A hobby, I knew, was something grown men were supposed to have. A hobby kept a man busy so he wouldn't be bothering his wife for sex. Elsie had told me this. I was fourteen that summer and kept close watch on my aunt and uncle's marriage for clues about what lay ahead. And a man needing a hobby was a crucial thing to know about married life.

"Management" was what Elsie called marriage: The State of Holy Management. She'd explained this to me many times. "Men don't know which end is up," she'd say. "They're clueless. But still, you've got to be kind. You don't want them going around thinking they've got no equipment. That's a recipe for trouble!"

"Pee-eew!" my friends squealed when I told them this. "Ballzzzzz!"

DURING ANOTHER SUMMER WE were driving up-Island on a family outing. As usual we weren't paying attention to the scenery. We were looking for the next sign – not the one with the litterbug – but the one we'd heard promised a glass castle constructed entirely of embalming-fluid bottles. It was somewhere past Duncan. That's where we were headed, a sweaty two-hour drive from Cordova Bay.

There were six of us jammed inside the Zephyr: Elsie, Ernie, Billy, Maudie, Grandma, and me.

Ernie was driving. He always drove because Billy liked to navigate, liked to estimate the times of arrivals and departures, the ETAs and

ETDs, liked to arrive at a destination without any hitches. He'd studied navigation at sea and could, if required, navigate by the stars.

"Never set your sights by the moon," he told me often, another of his Truths about Life.

Elsie was squished between Ernie and Billy in the front seat. "Shoot, we're stuck together like pigs," she laughed, pulling a damp arm away from Ernie's shoulder. Her flesh was as white as lard.

In the back seat Grandma hummed nursery rhymes, tapping time with her feet, which were perched on the hump between the seats. Maudie sat on one side of Grandma; I sat on the other.

We were travelling along, and I remember feeling mildly content. Usually the prospect of a drive with my strangely configured family brought a flat-out refusal. But not this day; I was as eager to visit the glass castle as everyone else. We'd heard there was a glass elephant's head attached to the outside wall, and a glass Coke bottle twenty feet high. There was even a gift shop.

"What's embalming fluid?" I hollered above the wind.

"It's used to make dead people look alive," Elsie said, twisting towards me. "For the funeral. They used it on Fred. Remember Fred, Ernie? He never looked so good. His skin was like wax."

Ernie grunted.

"I can't see it," Billy said. "Using embalming-fluid bottles to make a castle. It doesn't make sense. There aren't enough dead people in these parts. They probably used pop bottles."

Grandma, meanwhile, sat clacking her false teeth. It was a pleasant sound, like a horse sauntering down a tree-lined street on a summer's day. A horse named Daisy wearing a straw hat.

After a while she hummed "Three Blind Mice."

Perhaps our casual habit of throwing garbage out the car window gave her the idea for what she did next. In one fluid movement she pulled the teeth from her mouth, reached across me, and flung them out the window. She did this as naturally as if she was getting rid of an empty chip bag. Vaguely, I wondered if Ernie would be pleased.

According to the sign we'd just passed, the teeth landed about ten miles south of the glass castle.

"Grandma's thrown her teeth out the window!" I screamed, delighted. "Back there by the sign."

Ernie screeched to a halt by the side of the road. A cloud of dust plunged into the car.

Elsie hung over the car seat and shrieked. "What did you do that for?"

Grandma's eyes darted about bright and mad. Then she shrugged. Then she sucked on her cheeks and her whole face collapsed.

Billy pushed his baseball hat back on his head and sighed. He pulled the pencil from behind his ear. Here was a hitch: his ETA would need revising.

"Oh, Ma," Maudie said, a wretched look on her face.

"Oh, Ma nothing," Elsie hissed. "I knew something like this would happen. Something always happens. Didn't I say those very words this morning, Ernie? Didn't I say, 'Just once I'd like to go someplace and have nothing happen?'"

"She should be in a home," Ernie said quietly, but everyone heard.

"Don't talk stupid," Elsie said. "We should put you in a home. You and the bloody TV set."

We were stopped by a farm field. Cars sped by, rocking the Zephyr.

I'd seen Grandma's teeth lots of times when I'd stayed over at Maudie's house – at night, on her bedside table. They lay at the bottom of a glass of water, top and bottom joined at the back like a set of castanets.

"Ernie!" Elsie suddenly shouted. "Turn the car around! We've got to find those teeth!"

Turning the car around was something Ernie was already doing. He shot Elsie a murderous look and asked her if she'd finally gone off her rocker.

Elsie gasped. "Of all the bloody –!"

I yelled, "Hurry up! The teeth might get stolen!" I don't know why I said this. I felt urgent, caught up in the drama.

Elsie told me to pipe down. Everything, she said, was getting on her nerves.

Ernie told us both to quit squawking.

Sweat was running down his face.

"Quit yer damn squawking," is what he said.

Right then and there I decided I was never getting married. Elsie and Ernie were not a good advertisement for married life. Marriage was a bad movie starring Bette Davis, who poisons her husband and then watches him die. They're on the porch of their house. "Not feeling well, darling?" Bette asks smoothly, eyes wide with fake innocence. Then stares placidly at her husband while he writhes at her feet.

"SLOW DOWN. THERE'S THE sign!" Billy yelled. He'd been watching the road like a lookout.

It was a homemade sign, white lettering on plywood: "Glass Castle – 10 Miles."

When the car stopped I was the first one out. We were parked beside a steep ditch. Beyond the ditch farmland stretched to a line of trees in the distance. The silence felt eerie.

"Sheesh!" Ernie said, hauling himself out of the car and looking around. "We're in the middle of nowhere."

Elsie got busy and emptied the car ashtray, heaping cigarette butts and ashes onto the roadside like an offering.

"Now what?" Ernie said, wiping his glasses with a hankie and casting an approving glance at his wife stooped over the road.

Everyone looked to Billy, the navigator, not Ernie, for instructions. Ernie's expertise was travelling garbage. But making decisions in a catastrophe? That was Billy's department.

Billy put one foot on the car bumper, shielded his eyes from the sun, and stared up and down the road. Waiting for what he had to say, we gazed about helplessly – at the dry fields, the bleached sky with its few wispy clouds.

Finally, he turned to us. "We'll have to find those teeth. You can head up there," he told Elsie and Ernie, pointing north. "Have a look in the grass by the side of the road." To me he said, "You and Maudie look the other way. I'll take the ditch by the sign." This was a sacrifice, we knew, because there was no way the rest of us could tackle the ditch: Elsie, Maudie, and me in dresses; Ernie because he was fat and broke out in a sweat when he climbed a flight of stairs.

Ernie grumbled. "Ma could at least look for her own teeth."

"That's the most ridiculous thing I've ever heard," Elsie snapped.

Which was true: Ernie was being ridiculous. Grandma was eighty-seven years old and gaga. Maudie said she had to watch her like a hawk. I often forgot she was Elsie's, Maudie's, and Billy's mother.

I watched Elsie start off in a huff. From head to toe she was peeved. Every time a car went by her dress flared up from her knees and she slapped at it angrily. Because of the heat, she'd rolled her stockings to her ankles. She stumbled along in high heels.

Maudie and I headed the other way. It was hot searching the roadside. There was the pounding sun, the dust and, between passing cars, that heavy silence. After we'd walked a quarter of a mile Billy waved at us to return.

When we got back to the car, he was sitting sideways in the passenger seat with his shoes and socks off picking gravel from between his toes. Elsie and Ernie were back and Elsie was pouring tea from the picnic thermos into six green plastic cups. She'd lined the cups on the hood of the car like a special hood ornament. Inside the car the teeth sat on the dashboard. Billy had found them at the side of the ditch, not far from the glass castle sign. There were chips out of several teeth, but the set was still joined. Maudie said finding the teeth was a miracle. Ernie said he'd walked up the road for nothing and Elsie told him to shut up or she'd throw something at him.

Then Maudie handed round the tin of cookies.

Grandma put a cookie to her mouth and stopped. "Where's my teeth?"

"You threw them out the window," Elsie said.

"I did not. You're always fibbing."

"Oh, forget it," Elsie said. "What's the point?" She got the teeth from the car and rinsed them with tea. "Here," she said, giving them to Grandma. "Put them in."

Grandma took the teeth. I heard the sucking sound as she put them back in her mouth.

Later that day we discovered that Grandma had left her purse behind at the glass castle sign, though nobody worried about this. The purse was old and stuffed with folded newspaper, something Grandma insisted on doing each time she left the house. We found it on the way home. Ernie shook it out right away. "'Nuff's 'nuff," he said.

We watched the newspaper blow across the nearby field.

"Looks like big confetti," said Elsie.

"Kinda beautiful," Maudie sighed.

And then we drove away.

[PORK CHOPS]

Elsie, Doreen, Shirley

It was no secret to me as a young teenager that Elsie's main job as a wife was to keep Ernie busy around the house and yard, keep him diverted so he wouldn't be prone to the sex-crazed eyes that all wives feared. Sex-crazed eyes, I knew by now, could happen in a flash if a woman wasn't vigilant. "Keep a man well fed and worn out," Elsie often said. "Then your life will be your own."

Having a life of your own was hard to reconcile with the pamphlet my friend Valerie and I found in her mother's drawer. We read it as our future and were appalled. "A woman's body belongs to her husband, so it's important to keep it clean and well-groomed." There was a drawing of a fully clothed woman lying like a corpse on top of a double bed. Her eyes were closed. She wasn't smiling. She was waiting – dutifully? resignedly? – for her sex-crazed husband to pounce on her.

"Oh, barf!" we screamed.

Still, if anyone could avoid that poor woman's fate it was Elsie. I'd often watch her going about the important work of keeping the beast at bay. But who could figure harmless old Ernie as a beast? Was he really prone to "urges"? And, like all men, did these "urges" cause him to lose his mind?

Ernie wore thick, black-framed glasses, and I became curious as to what lay behind them. It was difficult to get a good look at his eyes because of the glasses but I wanted to get a reading, see if his eyes were even remotely sex-crazed, though I wasn't sure what sex-crazed eyes look like. Wild? Mean? Insane? Bugged out?

I found an opportunity to make an observation one afternoon while he was watching *The Three Stooges*. Joining him for the show, I dropped my bag of chips at his feet so I could get a close look at his eyes while picking it up. Nose to nose I peered through his smudged glasses.

"Whatcha doin?"

"Nothing."

"Well, quit it. You're giving me the creeps."

Ernie eyes were disappointing. They were dull brown in colour, and about as crazed looking as a puppy's. But then maybe Ernie was simply exhausted, the result of Elsie's successful campaign. He was too pooped to do anything but drag on his cigarette, stare at the TV.

I wondered further. What about sex-crazed behaviour? What did *that* look like? Constant drooling? Chasing Elsie around the house with his tongue hanging out when I was at school? Acting like an ape?

As far as I knew Ernie did none of these things. But maybe there were other less obvious signs that I didn't know about. Watching my squat bald uncle in his grey janitor's clothes going about his regular life – taking out the garbage, washing the outside windows, sucking on a piece of Cadbury's chocolate – I couldn't imagine what these other signs might be. True, he often licked his full purplish lips. But this wasn't drooling. This was because he had something stuck to them – pieces of chocolate, tobacco, cookie crumbs, cat hair, peas, and, once, a small dust bunny.

Elsie had a war going against Ernie and the TV set. She must have decided that too much TV meant the sex fiend that lived inside him was resting up, gaining enough energy to pounce on her when she least expected it. She must have been constantly looking over her shoulder while she worked at the sewing machine, or scrubbed the kitchen floor on her hands and knees, or planted Naughty Mariettas in the border alongside the house. This would explain why she was frequently on edge: she was on the lookout in case Ernie's beast reared its ugly ... pee-eew! I always stopped there.

This is how she operated. Ernie would be plunked down with his chocolate bar in front of the TV set before supper, grinning away at the show, oblivious to everything except *Mighty Mouse Playhouse*, when Elsie would suddenly bawl, "Ernie! The grass needs cutting!" "The garbage!" "What about the drainpipes?" "There's an ants' nest in the basement!" "The sink's plugged!"

We never knew for sure when she'd go off, but you could pretty well count on it happening any time Ernie was still – drinking tea, watching cartoons, hiding out in his workshop. Her screaming raised neck hairs and stopped hearts. Before the TV Ernie would jolt as if he'd been smacked and then, shuddering, resettle in his chair, light up another cigarette, take a long, weary drag, blow smoke rings, pick the stray bits of tobacco from his lips, and then, with a heavy sigh, try to re-enter Mighty Mouse's universe. None of this was of any use.

"Well?" Elsie would bellow from the doorway.

"Well what?" he'd answer hopelessly.

"I can't make supper with a bloody sink that's plugged."

And then he'd heave himself from his chair and head out the front door.

"Where are you going?"

"To get my tool box," he'd growl, barely audible. "Or do you think I can fix the sink with my bloody teeth?"

WEIRDLY, ELSIE AND ERNIE'S last name was Sexton. It was right there in the phone book: E. Sexton. Kids and panting men were always calling us up. "Got any sex for sale?" "Is this the *sex* house?" We became adept at slamming down the receiver whenever we heard pipsqueak giggles or heavy breathing on the other end of the line. Heavy breathing, another clue?

I thought that having sex in their name was a riot because, as far as I knew, Elsie managed Ernie so well that they never did it. He was too exhausted – up at five every morning to get to the library by six; all those household chores he had to complete, day in, day out. My bedroom was next to theirs and all I ever heard was snoring and the odd yelp from Ernie.

"Keep stubbing my toe," he'd say, when I'd ask about the yelp.

But more than sex-crazed men, and sex, in particular – which terrified me, both the badly understood mechanics of it and the disastrous life-ruining result if you got knocked up – I yearned to know first-hand about love and romance. Surely this was something that existed – like a placid meadow hidden within a forest that you'd unexpectedly come upon and be delighted with. Even though I didn't see romantic evidence between the men and women in my family – the only kisses were demure pecks at Christmas or birthdays, no one held hands, no one uttered the word "love" – I was desperate for proof.

Elsie's usual comment on the subject of romantic love was to snort. "Hah! Only in the movies. Real love's nothing to write home about. It's a two-faced beast. Sweet before the wedding to lure you in. Cranky for the next forty years."

Elsie's views were supported in chorus by Doreen; by her other married daughter Shirley who was living in California and presumably spreading the word down there; by Grandma before she'd gone gaga; and by Maudie.

I HAD THE OPPORTUNITY to ask questions about love one stormy Saturday afternoon in November when Doreen, Grandma, and Maudie were visiting. We were having tea in the kitchen when Elsie started in on her favourite topic.

"Men. You're damned if you do and damned if you don't," she declared. "There's no pleasing them. I've about had it up to here." She sliced her neck viciously with her hand.

What had ticked her off – again – was Ernie. He'd gone off pork chops. "You try to give them what they like, and they turn on you," she said.

"How?" I asked, the eager disciple.

"They make a sour face and act hurt," she answered, suddenly changing gears, telling the story like a joke. We were all ears. "How was I supposed to know he'd gone off bloody pork chops? Pork chops have always been his favourite supper. But do you think he'd say something? Do you think we'd have a conversation about it? Oh no, not him. Keeps his trap shut. I'm supposed to be a mind reader. That's me, Madam Elsie, the mind reader with a crystal ball."

Everyone laughed except Grandma. She was playing solitaire at the end of the table and looked up when she heard the rest of us laugh. "Ha, ha, ha," she said, the words keeping time with the nursery rhyme she'd been humming, "Pease Porridge Hot."

"Two bloody pork chops!" Elsie continued. "Last night at the supper table. Fried just the way he likes 'em. With the fat all burned. There he was, poking and picking at 'em like they'd gone bad. Putting his nose to the plate and sniffing. Like this."

She demonstrated for us, bending over and sniffing the tabletop. Doreen let out a scream.

I'd been at the pork-chop supper but didn't remember the sniffing part. What I did remember, though, was (unspoken) Rule Number One: Anything for a laugh; anything for a good story.

"He acted like I was trying to poison him," Elsie continued. "'What's the matter with you?' I said. And he looked at me like he'd just pulled his head out of a garbage can. His face all pinched and snooty." Here

Elsie scrunched up her face in another imitation and nodded her head, side to side, while everyone laughed some more.

"What happened next?" I asked.

"I'm getting to it," she said. "Don't rush me." (Rule Number Two: Take your time.) "He just looked at me like I was a blank wall, and said, 'I'm sick of pork chops.' Just like that. 'You're sick of pork chops? Well, thanks for telling me,' I said. 'You could have let me know.'" Here Elsie changed her tone, became thin-lipped, severe. "Now he won't talk to me. Gone out to his bloody shop. He can move the cot out there for all I care. Go live in his shop. Cook his own bloody meals. I've been getting the silent treatment since last night."

Doreen, married for six years by now and Elsie's main confidante, said resignedly, "Makes you mad when they do that."

Elsie stubbed out her cigarette and took up the teapot for pouring. "Damn right it makes you mad. For two cents I'd chuck him in the ocean. I'd chuck *all* men in the ocean. What's the good of 'em?"

I could swear the house shook after this declaration, but it may have been the storm. It continued unabated outside the kitchen window with lashing rain, screaming gulls. Ernie had built our small house; it was perched rather dramatically on the cliffside overlooking Cordova Bay. This was fine in summer when the view was spectacular and the weather balmy, but because the house was so exposed it bore the brunt of winter storms; the wind blew mercilessly through the cracks around the windows in the sea-facing front room. Elsie combated this problem by hanging grey wool blankets across the doorless opening, the result being that most of the house's natural light was shut out as well.

That afternoon all the lights were on in the house and the electric heat was cranked up past eighty, though the kitchen thermometer said sixty-eight.

Grandma, meanwhile, had started a whispery chant, "Ha, ha, ha." She was standing now and drawing circles on the steamed-up kitchen window. "Ha, ha, ha," got her halfway down a circle, then another "Ha, ha, ha," got her to the top.

Elsie ignored Grandma's background music and carried on talking. "Butter wouldn't melt in his mouth when I've given him pork chops before. Why the change all of a sudden?" She lit another cigarette. We watched the smoke drift across the cookie plate.

"It's different when you're in love, isn't it?" I said to the table.

Three faces looked at me with frank astonishment.

"What do you mean?" Elsie asked, suspicious.

"Love. When you're in love. It's different than with pork chops, isn't it? It's all ... I don't know ... good."

Doreen immediately went dreamy.

Elsie said, "Hah!" But she was thinking it over. "The beginning part's okay," she conceded. "I'll give you that. The flowers and nice manners. The way they fall over you like cocker spaniels. But it don't last. It never does. The bloom is soon off the rose."

Maudie, who never said much about men except to nod helplessly when the subject came up, was now smiling inwardly. "I had a lovely wedding," she said at length. "I made the dress myself. I even sewed pearls on the bodice." She turned to Elsie and laughed. "Remember the bagpipes? I walked down the aisle to bagpipes!"

Doreen's face lit up. "We had a dance band at my wedding. You had a little yellow dress," she said, turning to me happily. "And little white shoes. Remember that, Marion? You were only eight years old."

Elsie let out an impatient sigh. "And it all ends up with being sick of bloody pork chops."

I asked, "What was your wedding like? To Ernie. Was there music? What did you wear?"

"There was no music," Elsie said briskly. "I wore a blue suit with a matching pillbox hat. Your father walked me down the aisle because Pa was drunk. What more do you want to know?"

"Did you go on a honeymoon?"

"We went to Seattle for the weekend. By boat. I got seasick."

"That must have been fun," Doreen said.

"None of it was fun. You were at Maudie's refusing to live with us after the wedding. I couldn't do a thing with you. You were awful. Said you'd rather die."

"I *was* awful," Doreen grinned. "I didn't like Pop at first." In the last few years, she'd taken to calling Ernie Pop.

"Then what?" I asked. "After the wedding."

"Then nothing. This house. You coming to live with us when you were five. The girls getting married."

She gave me a level look. "What's all this talk about love, anyway? What's going on?"

"Nothing. I was just wondering."

"Well, don't bother. It never pays to get moony over a man. Every minute of every day some stupid girl is being hoodwinked by the promise in a Valentine's Day card."

"Valentine's Day only comes once a year," I said, happy to trip her up.

"Don't be ridiculous," she said. "You know what I mean."

There was a rare lull then around the table. Rain continued pelting the house. The clouds were so low and dark you couldn't see the ocean. Gusts of wind buckled the windows.

"Look there's Mr. Magoo," Doreen cried. All of Grandma's circles had cleared the window of steam and we could see out.

Ernie's pet seagull was perched shakily on the clothesline pole near the side of the house; he wobbled in the wind. Ernie fed him bread crusts every day after work. When the seagull saw Ernie it would fly down and patter towards him on thin pink legs.

I wondered now about Ernie in his workshop, and what he was doing. He had an electric heater in there; he had his chocolate bars, his silver foil. He was probably making airplanes, I decided, though the thought of him flying them while a storm raged outside was sad – the brief ascent, the nosedive onto the cement floor. I wondered briefly about the men in the family. Did they find the women as awful as we apparently found them? Ernie, Bob, Kenny Pepper – he was always called by both his names – Billy when he was over. They seemed happy enough, watching *Wide World of Sports* together on Saturday afternoons, passing around the bowl of Cheezies, filling in the long stretch until supper.

"Mr. Magoo's hungry, I said. "Ernie hasn't fed him today."

"There's an idea," Elsie said, cheering up. "I'll put Mr. Magoo in a stew. See how his lordship likes that!"

Doreen chortled, but I screamed, "Elsie!"

Maudie bit into a cookie and then spoke. "When Frank was alive, I rolled his cigarettes for him every night. And put them by his side of the bed so he'd have one when he woke up. One night I didn't make enough and he nudged me in the ribs. 'I'm out of fags,' he said. So I got up at three in the morning and rolled him four more."

"I would have shoved the bloody cigarettes down his throat," Elsie said. "Why you put up with it I'll never know. The way you ran after him. But that's men for you. Think of no one but themselves."

Maudie shrugged and grinned sheepishly. "Oh well," she said.

Doreen patted her hand. "Uncle Frank was a good provider," she said loudly, as if to a deaf person. "He left you well off, didn't he? You've got his navy pension. The house all paid for."

"Umm," Maudie said.

Grandma said, "Ha, ha, ha, ha, ha," only louder now, stomping her feet up and down in a stationary march.

"Oh, Ma, put a sock in it," Elsie said.

Grandma stuck out her tongue and continued stomping.

"Maybe Ernie's sick," Maudie suggested kindly. "Maybe that's why he couldn't eat the pork chops."

"Oh, you don't think so, do you?" Doreen added, worried. She cried easily. Already her eyes were brim full.

"Sick, my eye!" Elsie boomed. "He ate half an apple pie last night watching TV. And that was before his bedtime snack!"

Clearing away the tea things her mood abruptly softened. "What about Ernie in the workshop?" she said. "He's pouted long enough. And it's cold out there. The shop heater don't always work."

"He'll turn into a Pop-sical," I said. "Get it?"

No one paid any attention to me. (Rule Number Three: Pick Your Moment.) All eyes were on Elsie.

"Want me to bang on the shop door? See if he wants tea?" Doreen asked.

"Can if you like. I'll put the kettle on for a fresh pot. But he better not mention pork chops again. Honestly, I could have spit," Elsie laughed, a sign that their fight was over, and turned towards the sink.

Ten minutes later we watched as Ernie took the offered cup of tea from Elsie. He looked harmless enough standing there in his slippers and old blue cardigan; there was no way I could imagine him being "sex-crazed." Beneath the glare of the kitchen light you couldn't see his eyes through his glasses, couldn't know what he was thinking. He said nothing to us, which wasn't unusual; he often acted wary before a group of women. Elsie had wedged four chocolate chip cookies around his cup and saucer, two more than his usual share. He took the cup without comment and padded off for the TV set in the den.

Elsie winked at us behind his back.

I was struck by that wink. Maybe she loves him after all, I thought. Maybe that wink is proof.

[BAKED SALMON]

Marion with Susan and Jimmy, Shirley's children,
outside Maudie's house

Right from the start Martin Defolio knew my
position on sex. Knew that I was saving myself, not for marriage, but
from the disaster of being knocked up. This terrible thing had recently
happened to Rhonda Tuttle. One weekend my girlfriends and I were
dancing at her pyjama party and the next she was crying her eyes out in a
home for unwed mothers. We were fifteen and this was 1962. Instantly,

Rhonda Tuttle's life was over. When she heard the news, Elsie said with relish, "Now maybe you'll understand what's what. You don't want to end up shit creek without a paddle like Rhonda Tuttle, do you? Her poor mother could just about die."

The thing was, shit creek had its attractions and, notwithstanding the certainty that sex would ruin my life, Martin Defolio was one of them. I'd met him the previous summer in front of Woolworth's department store while working part-time as an ambassadorette, one of three girls hired to promote Victoria's centennial: 1862–1962. He was standing with two other guys sharing a cigarette. The sun was shining on his stiff, curvy hair; he was tall and skinny and wore a slouchy black-and-brown striped sweater over stovepipe pants; he gave me a cynical and weary smile when I stared at him. On top of that Martin Defolio oozed *bad*. My impression was confirmed when Nadine, one of the other ambassadorettes, who was a Victoria girl, said his brother was in jail.

We were dressed in grey slacks, high heels, red-velvet tailcoats, and grey top hats. "Buy a booster button? Support Victoria's centennial?" we'd holler at passersby. We looked like hat-check girls in the movies with our trays of buttons slung around our necks, our top hats tilted over one eye. I asked Martin Defolio that day if he wanted one of my buttons. He smiled ... slightly, licked his narrow lips, then looked at his friends and winked. Finally, he tossed a quarter onto my tray and asked for my phone number. I wrote it on the back of his cigarette package.

I lied to Elsie about Martin Defolio's age. Otherwise I wouldn't have been allowed to date him.

I said he was sixteen.

I said he was on the honour roll at school.

I said he wanted to be an accountant when he grew up, like Mr. Holt next door who was so rich he took his family to Hawai'i for two weeks every Christmas.

Elsie liked the idea of my dating a future rich boy. She said, "Well, isn't that nice. We'll have to invite Martin to dinner."

Alarmed, I told her he didn't eat dinner. Only mashed carrots and milkshakes, that he had a problem with his stomach. I didn't want her inspecting him up close.

Elsie called him a poor skinny thing and asked if he maybe ate fish. I said I didn't think so, that he fed himself with a tube.

Elsie said, "Is that a fact?"

After a couple of dates I got to know what Martin Defolio was like. He may have been good-looking and owned a car – a lowered Mercury splattered with orange primer – but he wasn't that smart. He was nineteen and still in grade ten at Victoria High School; they kept him for the basketball. And he was incapable of speaking in distinct words. "Wazzawannado?" he'd ask.

I soon started replying in a similar fashion: "Idunnowhachoowannado?"

But conversation wasn't the point of Martin Defolio; the point was being seen in a car with an older boy from Victoria, with someone who was the exact opposite of the buzz-cut twerps at my Cordova Bay school, a place that qualified as the boonies.

The point was impressing my friends. To them I started calling Martin Mr. Puke. This was because during each "date" while parked at the White-Spot drive-in he'd get drunk on vodka and Orange Crush and throw up out the car window. Chunks of cheeseburger and fries would splash onto the sides of his car, the drive-in parking lot, the pavement of Douglas Street. Sometimes he'd try to get in my pants and *then* throw up. This was not a comment on my performance. There was no performance. There was only barf. We'd be parked up at Mount Tolmie overlooking the lights of Victoria with all the other fogged-up cars bouncing away nearby, and Martin would get slobbery. His bony hand would start crawling up my leg, an inch at a time, as if this was war (it was!) and his hand was a creeping soldier with a grenade gripped between his teeth.

"My aunt was right," I'd later shriek to my friends, relating another tale of fighting off the beast. "All a guy wants to do is to haul out his gearshift and ruin your life!"

After taking me home weekend nights – I had an 11 p.m. curfew – Martin drag raced down Yates Street in Victoria. There was a front-page story in the *Victoria Daily Times* complaining about this. Martin and his friends, though unnamed, were called a gang of juvenile delinquents.

"It's not the same guy," I told Elsie after she'd read the story and was looking at me with narrowed eyes. "It's someone else."

I took the newspaper to school. "That's *him*! That's *him*!"

SOON AFTER, ELSIE DECIDED it was time to invite Martin to Sunday dinner. I tried to thwart the invitation by citing his "eating problem" but Elsie was determined. She asked him herself on a Friday night when he picked me up for our usual drive and park and puke at the White Spot.

Dinner was to be baked salmon, a dish that nobody in my family liked. But we were having it, Elsie told me pointedly, because I'd given her the idea that fish was the only thing that Martin Defolio could eat. A lot of trouble went into preparing the meal – cookbooks were checked, phone calls made. How many minutes per pound in the oven? Covered or not?

With the salmon we were having mashed potatoes, frozen peas, and turnips and carrots, also mashed. A bowl of lemon wedges sat on the table beside the rectangle of margarine. The best knives and forks and plates were used for the settings, the best paper napkins.

At four thirty I hung around the kitchen. "How much longer?" Martin was the first boy I'd ever had to supper and I was nervous, not only because there was a good chance my lie about his age and his eating habits would be discovered, but because I didn't like him very much by then and worried that my family would think we were in love.

Elsie said, "What's the rush?"

Doreen, who along with Bob and three-year-old Lyn had dinner with us every Sunday, smirked and nodded towards the den where Martin was watching TV sports and drinking beer with Ernie and Bob. "He's a big hit!" she said.

Elsie agreed, sounding pleased. "It's like old home week in there. And he's such a nice boy. So polite. Not anything like a juvenile delinquent."

All I could do was groan.

We sat down to eat at twenty to six, late because Elsie wasn't sure the fish was cooked. Bowls of food were set out on the table, something that was not usually done; supper was always dished up at the stove.

We were eating at the grey Arborite kitchen table with the chrome legs. The top of it was designed to look like marble. Everyone had a full glass of milk before them.

Martin Defolio and I sat on one side of the table; Doreen, Bob, and Lyn were jammed on the other side; Elsie and Ernie sat at either end. I was expecting someone to say grace, as a joke. This often happened at "formal" meals: "Grace? Grace? Anybody seen Grace?" "She's not here! She moved to Podunk, Saskatchewan!" But this didn't happen.

Then I was afraid someone would look in the window and see Martin and me sitting side-by-side like a married couple and split a gut and tell everyone at school and then the whole school would split a gut.

When we had the napkins placed on our laps Bob hollered, "Pass the smashed potatoes," spreading his grin around the table like the goofball he was.

Elsie said sternly, "Pass Martin the food first." Everyone did. He sat bewildered with three bowls and the salmon platter in an arc before him while the rest of us stared, watching what he'd take first. He took the peas.

Then Ernie opened up the dinner conversation. "They're calling for snow."

Elsie said happily, "I love snow. One time when I was a kid we skated outdoors." She'd taken off her apron. She wore one of her good dresses, the purple crepe with the fancy stitching on the bodice, as befitted a "special occasion." She had on her rhinestone glasses.

"How do you skate in snow?" Ernie asked sarcastically, catching Bob's eye. He ambushed Elsie every now and then when strangers were around and she couldn't be her true self and scream at him to go jump in the lake.

"Never mind," she said briskly. "I'll bet Martin likes snow."

He had a mouth full of potatoes and nodded eagerly.

"I'd still like to know how you skate in snow," Ernie said, persistent, eyeing Bob in triumph.

"Go look it up in a book. Since you're so *interested*." Elsie said, with a glance that indicated terrible things would happen to Ernie, later on.

Bob said, "Heh, heh, watch out Pop! You're gonna get it now!"

Doreen cried, "Bob! Mind your manners," and punched him in the shoulder.

Lyn screamed, "Skating! I wanna go skating!"

Ernie pretended he hadn't heard any of this. He had a pea stuck to the side of his cheek; it didn't fall off while he continued chewing and remained there when he pulled a fish bone from his mouth.

"You've got a pea stuck on your face," Elsie said sharply.

"Good," Ernie said, grinning nastily. "Do you want it?" He grazed his cheek with his hand. The pea fell on the floor, and he winked at Martin, who was feeling right at home. That was the main thing as far as the rest of them were concerned. Forget about snow. Forget about Ernie and the stuck pea. Martin Defolio was winning all the points. He was acting like he belonged. His jacket was slung across the back of his chair, his sleeves were rolled up his skinny arms like he meant business, he'd loosened his tie. Martin was a "dear" and "a good egg" and an "all right guy." He was such a success that I had the sick feeling he'd be invited for Christmas dinner. There could be nothing worse.

"Martin," Elsie now said, "I hear you plan on being an accountant." When Martin looked dumbfounded, she pressed on. "Like Mr. Holt next door. He's an accountant. And very well off, too." She stared pointedly at Ernie while she spoke meaning, we knew, "unlike *you* with your janitor's job."

"Huh?"

I held my breath.

"An accountant. Marion tells me you've got a head for figures."

"I bet he does," Bob cracked. "Eh, Marty? Va-va-va-voom." He pulled his shirt out from his chest. "Get a load of these knockers!"

"Oh, Bob," Doreen said wearily, "don't be such a moron."

"Voom voom," Lyn squealed.

Beside me Martin grinned at everyone and steadily pushed food into his mouth, including the salmon. Before long he choked on a fish bone. It seems he didn't know you weren't supposed to eat them. He coughed and coughed and his face turned red. Elsie jumped up and got a piece of bread and told him to swallow it, which he did, but not before Bob had given him several hard slaps on the back and Ernie had cried out, "Oh, heck!" and glanced, panic-stricken, at the phone in the hall. "Shouldn't we call an ambulance?"

"Don't be bloody ridiculous," Elsie said, forgetting her company manners in the midst of the catastrophe. "The bread will work just fine."

After Martin had swallowed the bone everyone laughed and congratulated him. Ernie said, "We thought you were a goner." Elsie gave him some sliced peaches and ice cream and said, "You won't choke on this, dear."

Then we had tea, weak as usual, because Elsie could never wait to pour it.

Martin Defolio left after *The Ed Sullivan Show*, which started at eight. Everyone insisted he watch it with us. I couldn't wait for him to leave but I was outnumbered. Seven of us were squeezed into the den. Martin sat chummily on the couch beside Elsie. I sat on the floor next to Ernie's chair, and Lyn sat on Ernie's lap. Doreen grabbed kitchen chairs for her and Bob.

The show began. There were acrobats and jugglers and a comedian to watch, an opera singer in the audience who was told to stand up and take a bow, the June Taylor Dancers lying on their backs making kaleidoscope designs with their legs. You watched them do this through a special camera mounted on the ceiling of the theatre. It was the highlight of the show. Then the show was over.

At the door Martin said, "Jawannagooutfridaynight?"

"I suppose," I said.

"Getchaseven?"

"Might as well."

Then he pulled his ring off his finger.

"Wannagosteady?"

I gasped.

Martin grinned. "Jawanna?"

I took the ring, a gold *M* set in black onyx. It was heavy. I could wear it on a chain around my neck like a trophy. Finally! All my girlfriends wore rings on chains, something that was a sore point with me; I was the only one who didn't. I'd wear the ring to school tomorrow, hanging outside my white sweater so everyone could see, a tiny hubcap banging triumphantly against my chest.

We kissed sloppily.

I pushed him away. "My aunt might see!"

Minutes later I was wailing down the phone line to my best friend, Dana.

"Mr. Puke gave me his ring!"

Dana squealed like this was the best news in the world.

The next day Elsie mentioned the baked salmon. "Dry as a popcorn fart," she said. "It was hardly touched. What a waste!" She gave me the evil eye.

"So much for Martin's special diet. Hah!" She put the salmon outside for the gulls.

TWO YEARS LATER, WHEN Martin Defolio was ancient history, I got a summer job working in the kitchen at the Butchart Gardens restaurant. There I learned from the Brentwood Bay farm women who were hired as summer cooks how to bake salmon. It's a simple recipe and the salmon is always moist.

When I tried the recipe for my family that summer Elsie picked at it. "Not bad," she allowed. "But then I've never been fond of fish. Must have been the fish heads my mother boiled for soup when I was a kid. The smell alone would kill you!"

Ernie agreed by asking the obvious, "Why would you want salmon when you can have roast beef?"

But I like it and use this recipe often.

BAKED SALMON
Whole salmon, sockeye or pink
Olive oil
Salt
Lemon slices

Fill cavity of salmon with lemon slices. Sprinkle with salt. Drizzle olive oil over inside and outside of fish. Wrap in tinfoil. Bake in a 325° oven for fifteen minutes a pound.

Ernie, Billy, Rip, Elsie

Miss Horel, our grade ten home ec teacher, was demonstrating how to sift flour. She stood before twenty girls, massive and inviolate in her handmade tweed suit with its handmade button-holes, while outside the sun shone, plum trees blossomed, and sullen older boys waited for us in souped-up cars. It was the last period on a Friday afternoon.

Miss Horel held the hand-cranked sifter over a sheet of wax paper and instructed us to turn to page ninety-one in our textbook, *Your*

Home and You. Here she read aloud. "In using flour for quick breads, sift before measuring."

"Write that down, girls," Miss Horel said. "And remember, the secret of light muffins is sifted flour." Then she paused to deliver her revelation. "Flour must be sifted not once, but *twice* if your muffins are to be light and airy! That's something you won't find in your textbooks." Which meant it would be a test question on the final exam. We wrote furiously.

It was 1963 and we all knew why we were there: we were housewives in training. Eventually a perfected version of Miss Horel's muffins would land in the mouths of our shirt-and-tie husbands, perhaps even into the mouths of the Larrys, Als, and Pats who were waiting outside at that very moment.

Muffin-making was difficult work, *scientific* work, we were told, and a vitally important skill to conquer if we were to ever take our places as confident homemakers of the nation. There were the exact measurements of baking powder, sugar, flour, and milk to consider, the crucial element of a well-greased muffin tin, the importance of lumpy batter.

There were six workstations in Miss Horel's class. Each station consisted of four girls seated around an Arborite-topped table. A bank of cupboards and drawers behind us was filled with our tools-in-trade – mixing bowls, muffin tins, cookie sheets, frying pans, and all manner of arcane utensils. We sat with our "Muffin Preparation Plans" before us wearing full white aprons with our names embroidered across the bibs.

We had sewn these rite-of-passage aprons in grade seven to mark the beginning of our domestic indoctrination. Ahead lay six years of learning increasingly difficult recipes, from pea soup in grade seven – *one can of peas, mashed, one cup of water, one cup of milk, salt and pepper to taste, and make sure you use a double boiler so the milk doesn't scald* – to macaroni and cheese, brown Betty, and poached eggs in grades eight and nine, and then on to the challenging shoulder cuts of meat in the higher grades. Marriage after high school was, of course, the intended climax of these earnest years, when *Your Home and You* would become reality. Marriage would transform us, we understood, into the smiling, high-heeled blond in the flowered apron that figured so prominently in our text books.

Miss Horel droned on. "When is a muffin done? What are the four tests? Lynne? Marion? Dana? Paulette?"

Consulting our books we read aloud, dutifully as opposed to sarcastically; there was no sense in irritating Miss Horel on a Friday afternoon: "The colour should be golden brown." "The muffins should pull away from the pan." "When you touch the top of the muffin with your finger the dent should spring back." "A knitting needle or a toothpick inserted in the centre of the muffin should come out clean."

Satisfied with our answers she instructed us to write them down as well.

"MUFFIN" WAS A WORD we used to mean small tits, so it was hard to keep a straight face during Miss Horel's demonstration. Using a kind of home-ec-Canadian-standard format, we graded our breasts the same way we had learned to grade eggs – from the smallest to the largest: "fried eggs," "muffins," "grapefruits," climaxing at the coveted "basketballs," meaning you were so stacked a boy's eyes fell out of his head when you passed by. Only one of my school friends had that distinction – the envied Paulette. Dana, Lynne, and I were solid muffins with maybe a slim chance of becoming grapefruits in later years. Miss Horel had basketballs, but her being a teacher, we didn't admire them.

School was Royal Oak Junior High. Grades eight to ten, 263 kids, thirteen teachers. Most of the men teachers were ex-military. The three women on staff – home ec, English, typing – were unmarried. The school served a wide area – the farmlands of Central Saanich, the suburbs of Royal Oak, and Cordova Bay, three miles away. Many of us took the school bus to get there. The school itself was made of cement blocks and set in a gully. In winter the gully became a swamp and the cafeteria flooded. We called the school Royal Joke.

MISS HOREL'S FIANCÉ HAD been killed in WW II and it was understood that she would remain husbandless forever. She was in her mid-forties then and we pitied her. She would never know the ecstasy of serving a perfect muffin to an appreciative husband, would never be the wife of any house, and worse, would have to eat her muffins by herself, getting bigger and bigger as the lonely years crept by.

"Always a bridesmaid, never a bride," Elsie said of her sadly. But there was a hint of disgust in her voice. Obviously Miss Horel was remiss in not tackling her situation more clear-sightedly. By pining for lost love, she had willfully and foolishly ruined her chances. "She could have found *someone*," Elsie said, as if spare men were waiting by the side of the road for Miss Horel to drive by and pick them up.

"There's lots of single men still living with their mothers who would appreciate a woman like Miss Horel, a good cook and homemaker," Elsie said. "Think what her old age will be like all alone. Always a fifth wheel at family dinners. Tagging along on drives." She shuddered.

"But isn't that how you got Ernie?" I asked. "Wasn't he a spare man living with his mother? Across the street from Grandma and Auntie Maudie's house?"

"Not the same thing! I was a widow with two small girls *and* I was on relief. When Sonny died of TB his family never lifted a finger to help," she added bitterly. "And Ernie had a steady job at the library and said he'd build me a house. And that's what every woman wants. A home of her own. And I got one."

"Oh."

"But what's the big deal," she scoffed, "about Miss Horel and those muffins? Dry old things. Even the seagulls won't touch 'em." Elsie's expertise was brownies and lemon squares and double-crusted pies.

Despite Miss Horel's grim domestic life, she was an enthusiast for housewifery, something we could never countenance given her old-maid status, even though teaching home ec *was* her job.

"Go figger!" we'd say to each another. If you couldn't have *Your Home And You* as your very own reality what was the point of menu planning? Of living? Why not kill yourself and be done with it?

MISS HOREL, LIKE ELSIE, was a maniac for cleaning, and this was also something she taught. In those days garbage may have been thrown out of car windows with abandon, but the ideal home was spotless. From Miss Horel we learned the secret of removing grime from walls, cupboards, and bathtubs – ammonia and dish soap – and how to scrub a floor on your hands and knees using vinegar and scalding hot water. We learned to use Lysol on toilets and sinks, spray Raid along baseboards in all seasons except winter, put perfume on dust rags so they would always smell sweet, and cover a broom with a dishtowel to sweep the ceiling for cobwebs. Not a speck of dust, not a scurrying bug, she told us, was allowed to take up residence in our future homes. We should, she said, be able to eat off our floors.

It sounded like slavery to me. I couldn't get over the fact that, as a future wife, I was expected to do all this – work. And not once in a while, but day in, day out, for years. This was what having a home of one's own meant? Eternal drudgery?

Elsie's housekeeping followed the spotless dictum, as did Mrs. Holt's next door, and Doreen's, and the houses of my girlfriends. They were part of the war-on-germs obsession that had overtaken women in the western world. Every household that I knew of was run along these lines. That is, except for Auntie Maudie's house. Hers was a testament to benign neglect, and in my mind she was a heroine and a rebel.

I loved that she let things in her fridge go mouldy, that milk got left out and soured, that canned peaches exploded in her basement, that dust gathered like tumbleweed beneath her bed, that cobwebs covered the aspidistra. When Elsie would tartly point out her house-keeping faults, Maudie would shrug her shoulders and laugh. She was too busy to bother, she'd say. There was the crossword puzzle to do, or her roses to tend to. There were letters to write to girlfriends in England that she hadn't seen in fifty years, or family pictures to sort through, or an interesting article in *Reader's Digest* to look at. Even though there were holes in her stockings and threads hanging from her skirt hem, I admired the fact that other things were more import-ant to her than housekeeping. Maudie's example meant that all the down-on-your-knees sweat over the kitchen floor that Elsie performed like a martyr – "No one appreciates the work I do!" – the constant mania about spots on the glasses, the windows, on your face, the way women lived in servitude to cleanliness, how it overtook their lives, was really not that important. Maudie proved this. Her house seemed fine to me. It was a celebration of barely controlled chaos. And, more importantly, Maudie was always happy. Hers was a relaxed household, more comfortable to be in than the usual spotless houses because you didn't have to constantly worry about where you put your glass, or if your shoes were wiped. At Maudie's house crumbs were scattered on the floors like confetti.

SOME OF US MADE notes that day while Miss Horel talked – Monday would be the actual muffin-making day – and some of us watched the institutional clock on the wall.

Miss Horel was also our guidance teacher and she had recently told us that it only took four minutes for a boy to destroy a girl's life. I wondered at the time, being without a husband, how she'd know this.

I'd watched the institutional clock on the wall above her desk after she'd made this announcement: the red second hand, the heavy minute hand, and the eternity they took to round the circle. Four minutes is a long time. I'd always thought your life would be ruined in an instant, say, if you drowned or were bashed on the head. But Miss Horel said four minutes; she was definite about this. Would the four minutes include kissing beforehand and the rumoured shared cigarette when it was all over?

It wasn't hard to picture Miss Horel peering through a steamed-up car window at Mount Doug on a Friday night with her sports-day stopwatch at the ready to time the four-minute dash: "Wait. Wait. Begin timing. Now!"

YEARS LATER MISS HOREL and her homemaking advice are still with me – in spite of my early resistance to them. Because, as it turned out, having a home of my own was something I really did want. Though its cleanliness has never reached Miss Horel's – or Elsie's – standard, it has approximated Maudie's. Thankfully, Miss Horel and high school home ec have come to my domestic rescue many times over the years, especially with her recipes for cheap and nutritious soups – boiled bones and vegetables – and the many things you can do with eggs. Her training in thrift has stood me well because, as it turned out, my husband and I were frequently broke. And, surprisingly, I find house cleaning to be a calming activity. There are times when, like Elsie, I would rather scrub a wall than have a conversation. Women didn't have yoga in hers and Miss Horel's day. But, actually, scrubbing a wall might amount to the same thing.

[VICTORIA'S ONLY TOE-TAPPER]

Left: Shirley, Top: Marion

When I was fifteen, I was billed as Victoria's only toe-tapper. This may or may not have been true. It was announced with three exclamation marks in Miss Blythe's dance recital program. "Three exclamation marks!!!" I told my friends. "I'm famous!"

Towards the end of the second act of *Stars of Tomorrow* the curtain closed and the Billy Tickle Orchestra in the pit at the Royal Theatre in Victoria played the opening bars of "Shuffle Off to Buffalo." This was my cue. Dressed in black-satin shorts, a matching tuxedo jacket, black fishnet stockings, and a top hat Elsie had made out of cardboard and painted black, I began my routine, a novelty act in front of the curtain while the stage behind was being prepared for the finale, an extravaganza number called Holiday in Rio involving the entire dance school.

My pointe shoes had special taps affixed to the toes, so that toe-tapping was like dancing on stilts. The routine consisted of pounding and hopping movements, several turns, and a couple of "breaks" which was a difficult step to do on your toes – one leg kicked back while balancing on the other. I thought I heard the audience gasp when I did the first one but the sound might have been Miss Blythe hissing at me from the wings. Throughout my performance she kept up a steady prompt: "Smile, goddammit, smile!"

Smiling while dancing, Miss Blythe often said, was personality, and personality would win the audience over every time.

Because of the lighting I couldn't see the audience – beyond the stage it was solid blackness – so it was hard to tell if my hopeful smiling was winning anyone over. The dance itself was like performing on the edge of a void, like grinning into nothingness, something a friend says I now do in a lot of my writing, akin to whistling in the dark.

That evening I proceeded on faith; somewhere out there Elsie, Ernie, and Billy were watching, maybe even thinking I was the next Judy Garland.

I loved tap dancing – the regular kind – the speed and abandoning fun of it. There was nothing like tapping to "Sweet Georgia Brown" played robustly in the practice room at Miss Blythe's downtown studio by her pianist, the elderly Irene. Five or six of us gleefully rehearsing the number while Irene, sweating at the keyboard, cheered us on: "That's it, girls! Now you're ripping up the boards!"

I'd been attending Miss Blythe's dance school for six years by the time I was singled out for toe-tapping stardom. She'd liked me well enough when I was younger and had long blond hair – she preferred her girls to look like fairy princesses – but at thirteen when it was cut short I was relegated to the back row in all the production numbers, to the no-girls-land where the inept, the unlovely, and the overweight were hidden. It was therefore a shock when she plucked me from dancing obscurity and had me fitted for toe taps. I wondered if she was punishing me in some way.

She was a demanding teacher and, to my mind, a ghoulish one. She seemed to like nothing better than pitting one girl against another; tears and hysteria were a common feature of her classes. "If you can't stand the heat get off the dance floor," she'd holler at some sobbing girl who'd just been told she pirouetted like a hippo. The admired girls were the ones with waist-length hair who half-fainted from overexertion and had to be helped to the bathroom where they could vomit demurely. These fainting girls, Miss Blythe told us, were examples of what "trying harder" meant.

She was in her fifties at the time of (what turned out to be) my one-and-only toe-tapping performance. A slim woman with tightly curled brown hair, she wore black pants, a black turtleneck, and ballerina slippers during our tap and ballet lessons. The rhinestones attached to the wingtips of her glasses gave off a malevolent glint when caught by the overhead lights. It was rumoured she'd once danced on Broadway, though Elsie sniffed when she heard this. "Show me the pictures! Where's the proof?"

In "real life," Elsie noted, Miss Blythe was a sad and lonely widow who lived by herself in a big empty house on the Dallas Road waterfront. Furthermore, she had no children. "Her students are her children," Elsie said, adding pathetically, "the poor thing."

Miss Blythe chain-smoked through our lessons, roaming the practice room with her cigarette and ashtray like a stalker on the lookout for bent backs and knock knees. "Stand up! Toes out!" she'd cry, then wheeze and cough. Amazingly, she lived to be a hundred.

WHILE MY TOE-TAPPING SOLO was nothing to write home about, as Elsie later remarked, Miss Blythe must have decided that I possessed enough "personality" to become one of her passing favourites because shortly after the recital she put forth Sherry's, Nadine's, and my names from her senior class to the Victoria Centennial Celebrations Society.

They were looking for three girls with "character" to help promote Victoria's centennial – 1862–1962. The three of us were to visit up-Island towns for ten days at the beginning of August – it was billed as a "Goodwill Tour" – with "Victoria's First Mayor," a man in his sixties called Sparky McFadden who'd be playing the part. Before that we were to sell centennial booster buttons on the streets of Victoria during the month of July.

The contract we signed with the Victoria Centennial Celebrations Society said we would be paid five dollars a day plus meals and accommodation for the trip, and twenty percent of all proceeds from the button sales, meaning we'd make five cents for every twenty-five-cent button we sold.

The Celebrations Society was housed in an empty store on Douglas Street next to People's Credit Jewellers. Inside there were only two tables, two chairs, two phones, and two crew-cut guys called Gary and Hank who were running things.

We were called The Ambassadorettes and I was allowed to go on the trip because it was "an official job," and because Miss Blythe had recommended me.

We didn't meet Sparky McFadden until the morning of the up-Island trip. I had sold three hundred and thirty-six booster buttons by then, earning a paltry sixteen dollars and eighty cents.

Sparky was a small man with a florid face and a short white beard which, as he made a point of telling us, was real. "Here, pull it!" he said – frequently. This was something, as I discovered in later years, that many men were fond of saying, and they didn't mean their beards.

Sparky wore an old-time mayor's costume and a black top hat. It was his car we'd be travelling in, a 1954 green Ford.

Before we left Gary – he looked like Bobby Darin – took me aside and gave me a fifty-dollar bill. "You look like the ringleader," he told me. "This is in case you get into trouble." Puzzled, I took the money.

For the first two days things were okay. As an official delegation we visited the Chamber of Commerce in Duncan and then dropped in on a woman's one hundredth birthday party. It was happening at the Kiwanis Club where a lot of people were standing around holding teacups. The old woman was sitting in an arm chair decorated with twisted green and yellow crepe paper, the kind of decoration done for bridal showers. When she saw the four of us in our costumes striding towards her she got scared and cried. We stayed long enough to have our pictures taken with her for the Duncan paper. The headline, when we saw it, read, "Two Centennials."

During those first days we met the mayors of Duncan, Lake Cowichan, Nanaimo, and Comox, visited a couple of old-age homes, a hospital, and Camp Thunderbird where a crowd of kids in wet bathing suits clamoured for booster buttons.

Between events Sherry, Nadine, and I lounged in the back seat of Sparky's Ford, him driving up front like a chauffeur. We lined our top hats in a row on the ledge behind the seat and shared movie magazines and comics and sang along to Motown hits on my transistor radio. I used part of the fifty dollars the organizer had given me to buy us potato chips, Cheezies, and bags of Scotch mints and jelly beans. We screamed at Sparky to stop for fries and Cokes every time we passed a coffee shop or a drive-in.

From our motel in Nanaimo, Sparky dropped us off at a movie – *Elmer Gantry* – and took himself to a bar.

The next morning, day three, we were on our way to Campbell River when Sparky began openly drinking rye from a brown-paper bag. He said we were driving him nuts. All our squealing and singing and talk about movie stars and makeup and hairdos was driving him "stark, raving bonkers."

"You sound like a bunch of crazed chickens. Squawk, squawk, squawk," said Sparky McFadden.

"You do that good," I said. "You sound like a rooster. Like an *old* rooster."

This made us laugh and start singing loudly, "They say that breaking up is har-ard to do-oo ..."

"I should have known," Sparky McFadden said, pulling at his beard and then guzzling from the paper bag.

"Now I know. Know that it's tru-oo ... Breaking up is ... har-ard to do-oou ..."

Around eleven o' clock he pulled over and turned to us. He was grinning and waving his fingers.

"Bye-bye," he slurred, and passed out across the seat.

For a while we sat there stunned and watched him snore. Then we felt disgusted.

"What a puke," I said, not knowing that puke in the form of Martin Defolio would soon become a big part of my life.

"Just a cruddy old drunk," said Nadine, who was a good tap dancer and could sing on stage like a cowgirl, "I'm an Old Cowhand from the Rio Grande ..."

"What shall we doooooo?" Sherry moaned. She was known for her backflips and the splits; "she's made of rubber," people said, awed. I, of course, was Victoria's Only Toe-Tapper (say no more).

Cars sped by. None of us could drive. Sherry was the oldest at seventeen but she didn't have her licence yet. Nadine was fifteen, the same age as me. There was nowhere to phone.

"So, what's the big deal?" I said, and climbed over the seat. I shoved Sparky's legs out of the way and started the engine. But didn't know how to use the clutch or change gears. The car kept stalling. Finally, I managed to lurch along in first. The car felt huge – what I imagined riding bareback on a bull would be like – wide and unwieldy. I drove mostly on the shoulder and then, gaining confidence, pulled onto the road – still in first gear – and got the speed up to thirty. But when a car passed, I panicked and swerved right, jerking to a stop down a ditch. The car shuddered, then wheezed. The top half of Sparky rolled onto the floor. He didn't wake up.

"Quick," I said. "Before someone comes."

We pulled and shoved him back onto the seat and propped him behind the steering wheel. Then we stood on the highway in our high heels and top hats. A woman driving by – "Oh, you poor things!" – took us to the police station where we were told we were lucky to escape with our lives. I used what was left of the fifty dollars for our bus ride home.

We told our families that Sparky got sick and the trip was cancelled.

That was the end of Victoria's first mayor and The Ambassadorettes.

LATER THAT SUMMER ELSIE, Maudie, Grandma, Doreen, Shirley, and Victoria's Only Toe-Tapper were sitting outside on the front patio facing the traffic of Cordova Bay Road. All of us, except Grandma, were wearing muumuus. It was the season of the muumuu, that baggy, shape-hiding dress from Hawai'i.

Shirley had arrived two days earlier from Sunnyvale, California, for a three-week holiday. She was twenty-five years old at the time and seven months pregnant with her third child. But you'd never know it because of the orange-flowered muumuu she was wearing. Unlike ours, which Elsie had made, Shirley's muumuu was store-bought and of a superior design and fabric. She looked sophisticated in her American clothes and wore sandals of a style we'd never seen before and now coveted – cork wedgies with the toes covered in pink plastic flowers.

Of the two sisters, Shirley was always referred to as the spunky one, the daredevil. Four years younger than Doreen, she had red hair and freckles. This feature, Elsie said, was the cause of Shirley's spunkiness and the reason she had "a mind of her own," meaning she did what she liked. As far as I understood, this was mainly to quit school at sixteen, marry young, move to California, and have all those kids, four things I vowed would never happen to me.

Unlike Shirley, no one ever called *me* spunky, so perhaps I needn't have worried. I was Miss Priss and Pus Lips (white lipstick), names that rendered me happily immune, I believed, from quitting school and marrying early. On top of this, Elsie often hooted, "Who'd want to marry you? Boys want nice girls. Not someone who traipses around with her nose stuck in the air like you do."

It seemed I was my family's version of *The Taming of the Shrew* because Elsie would invariably add with glee, "You just wait. You'll get knocked down to size."

That afternoon on the patio Maudie was sitting quietly nearby and paying warm and benevolent witness to the splendour that was the rest of us, as she always did. We counted on her seeing us this way. You could only be wonderful in Maudie's eyes, because Maudie loved everyone. Which was a fault, Elsie said, especially when it came to

Frank, her long-dead husband, and her only son, Kenny Pepper. He was, Elsie said, what Maudie lived for.

"But he doesn't appreciate what she does for him," Elsie would always add righteously. "Won't get out of bed till three in the afternoon. Poor Maudie has to lug the garbage cans to the end of the driveway herself. And don't even get me started on the way she waits on him hand and foot!"

For this reason we felt sorry for Maudie. She may have been a saint, but she suffered in silence, the only dignified thing a woman could do. This silent suffering was the truth, Elsie said. It explained Maudie's continual smiling. She smiled to hide her pain.

That day Maudie was smiling as usual. She was wearing a muumuu that had purple flowers on a hot-pink background. Elsie had made it for her birthday because Maudie would never sew a muumuu for herself. Housedresses, cardigans, and oxford shoes were what she wore. Elsie, however, deemed it one of her many missions in life to educate her dowdy sister about style. You were supposed to wear rubber thongs or high heels, or like Shirley, wedged sandals, with a muumuu but Maudie would not. She couldn't be persuaded to give up her black oxfords; she wore them with her muumuu without stockings. Her bare legs were disgracefully white, with gnarly dark varicose veins wandering across her shins, and her feet had bunions, as did Elsie's, lumps of bone and flesh sticking out below their big toes which probably explained why they hobbled when they walked.

Elsie looked at Maudie and sighed – it was hopeless! – and exchanged eye-rolls with Doreen and Shirley. But Maudie seemed oblivious to this. On the patio that day she was sitting on her hands, swinging her short legs, and beaming at us. We're wonderful, her shining eyes told us, too wonderful for words.

Shirley was lounging on one of Ernie's homemade deck chairs alongside Doreen. She was in a bad mood. Tired, she said. "I could sleep for a whole bloody year," she yawned. She sounded like Elsie; there was that edge. Her children, Susan and Jimmy, aged four and three, were playing in the new sandbox on the grass beside the patio. Doreen's three-year-old daughter Lyn was with them. They had pails and shovels and, for the moment, were quiet; no whining or crying came from their direction and it was blissful.

All these little kids, I was thinking, watching them with dismay. It was all anyone ever talked about. They were cute, all right, I gave them that, but I hated babysitting them. I hated babysitting, period. I was not one of those teenage girls driven to childcare. I was never going to have children. From what I could see it was all work and no fun. And marriage was even worse. I was sitting there, considering these things while painting my nails. I had plenty of examples to judge from, I continued musing. Shirley's marriage for starters. Her husband Ken hadn't come on this trip; he'd stayed in California. Everyone was glad about this because Ken was a shouter. He shouted at his kids – just babies! – and he shouted at Shirley. Also, he drank. He was a bartender so he drank, that was the explanation. I thought Ken was mean and wished Shirley had never married him. Now I was hoping she'd leave him and move back home. I'd put up with the kids just to have her here. I'd make myself stand it for Shirley's sake.

Elsie was talking about this very subject, something she'd been doing nonstop since Shirley arrived. "Move back home," she urged her again. "Ernie'll fix up the basement. You can stay here. Till you get settled."

But Shirley was giving her an argument. "How would I live? The baby's due in November. I can't go out to work."

"You can get welfare," Elsie said. "I did. When your father was in the sanitarium, I didn't have a choice. I made do with thirty-seven dollars and fifty cents a month. And the family will help."

I gave a laugh.

"What's so funny?" Elsie said. "Think you're too good for us?" She turned to the others. "Gets a toe-tap solo and thinks she's the Queen of Bloody Sheba."

"Thirty-seven dollars and fifty cents. Big deal," I said. "What could you buy with that?"

"It was plenty. You don't know what you're talking about."

"Excuse me," Shirley butted in, peeved. "I *have* a choice. About moving back. Ken's got a steady job and he says he'll stop drinking. Besides, I like it in Sunnyvale."

"You like those friends of yours," Elsie snapped. "Barb and Bob. They're not your family. They won't be there for you when things get tough."

"Things won't get tough," Shirley said.

"How can you stand Ken?" I added. "The way he screams at everyone?"

My comment hung in the air, fizzing out by the second. No one was interested in what I had to say. Elsie and Shirley were the stars of this conversation.

And it had clearly gone on long enough because Elsie next loaded and fired her biggest gun. "Well, you'll never see Grandma again if you stay in California. She'll be dead by the time you decide to come back."

Shirley looked at her mother in horror.

"See if I'm not right," Elsie said. "She's eighty-eight years old. How much longer do you think she's got?" The oracle had spoken.

Doreen, the beautiful *and* the sensitive one, started crying. Grandma was sitting on a kitchen chair in the shade of the carport roof staring at the road and counting the cars going by. She turned to us and said, "Thirty-two," and Doreen let out a sob. Maudie shrugged her shoulders and looked hopeless; Shirley scowled at her mother; Victoria's Only Toe-Tapper applied another coat of pink-pearl nail polish. Only Elsie, having rested her case, looked pleased.

I was wondering, "What now?" when one of the kids screamed. Sand had been thrown, or one of them had fallen, or one of them had messed their pants. It was always something; you never knew the cause. But the howling was the same. And contagious. One cried, they all cried.

Later, when things had settled down – food given, different toys offered – and we were having tea, Elsie came up with a bright idea. "I know," she exclaimed. "Let's go shopping!"

In an instant I saw what was coming and started gathering up my nail-polish things.

"What we need is a trip to the Town and Country Mall," Elsie said. "That'll cheer everyone up. There's a sale of towels on! And Ingledew's is having a shoe sale!" To Maudie she said, "You love a sale, don't you? We can drop you and Ma home on the way back."

But I wasn't invited; I was needed to babysit.

"Sorry," I said, getting up. "I'm busy."

"We'll pay you," Doreen hastily offered.

"No," I said, glowering at her. "Wild horses couldn't make me."

"Oh, please," Doreen begged. "Shirley won't be here for long. It'll be a treat for her to get away from the kids. We'll only be gone a couple of hours."

"I told you I'm busy. I'm going down the beach." I headed into the house to get my towel.

Behind me Elsie hollered, "There she goes. Victoria's One and Only – Pain in the Ass."

I turned around. Everyone looked gloomy. Then one of the kids screamed. Over the howling Maudie said, "Oh well, maybe it's a phase."

"Phase, my eye," Elsie snorted. "Doreen and Shirley were never this bad. They always did what they were told in the end."

"Until now," Shirley said.

[ACKNOWLEDGMENTS]

With love and thanks for permissions given:
Elsie Sexton, Doreen Jones, Bob Jones, Shirley Taillefer, Doris
(Jones) Talma, and Jenny (Holt) Pite. My thanks also to Kevin
Williams, Vicki Williams, Catriona Strang, and Leslie Smith of
Talonbooks for the twentieth anniversary edition, to Lynne Van
Luven for her generous introduction, and to Rob Sanders of
Greystone Books for the 2004 edition.

M.A.C. Farrant is the award-winning author of over twenty works of fiction, nonfiction, and memoir, and two plays. She has published ten books with Talonbooks, including her trio of miniature fiction *The World Afloat* (2014), *The Days* (2016), and *The Great Happiness* (2019). Her recent nonfiction books include *One Good Thing: A Living Memoir* (2021), a BC bestseller, and *Jigsaw: A Puzzle in Ninety-Three Pieces* (2023). She lives in North Saanich, British Columbia.